Bicycle Kicks

published in Great Britain by

18 Yeend Close
West Molesey,
Surrey KT8 2NY

www.GJBpublishing.co.uk
@GJBpublishing

Printed in Great Britain by
www.lulu.com

© Simon Hood 2012

Cover and illustrations by
Lee-Ann Donaldson
www.lee-anndonaldson.com

Bicycle Kicks logo designed by
Michael Elgie

Dla Joli

CONTENTS

FOREWORD

Being a York City fan is tough enough as it is, even if like me you mainly follow their progress sitting on the sofa in the living room waiting for live updates on the BBC website. In the thirty years I have supported them there have been a handful of occasions where a York City fan can feel like a winner, but if you want glamour and trophies or anything other than almost perpetual disappointment, then you can take the easy way out and support Chelsea or Man City or Man United. Following the Minstermen is an exhausting and unrewarding experience. Occasionally they will even start to play well and give you hope that something brilliant might be about to happen, only to (nearly always) pull the rug away at the last possible minute. In fact I have become so used to being let down that any periods of success leave me unable to cope. What are these emotions I am feeling? Happiness and pride in my team?
I have no way of knowing. There is nothing to compare them with.

Even deciding to go and watch every single game they play in a season is masochism on a par with Thomas A Becket's hair shirt. The pain is more real if you're there to see the results go against you in the snow and rain. So to choose to cycle to each game would take either incredible mental strength or otherwise be undertaken by someone who has already lost all their marbles and doesn't know any better. I don't know which camp Simon Hood started his challenge in, or indeed which he ended it in, but sane or mad he has to be applauded for his dedication and commitment and his belief in a team which has given so little cause for any of us to believe in them.

But when failure is your daily bread, then success can be as glorious as a glass of water to a man dying of thirst. Would Simon's Herculean task be rewarded with a rare and wonderful victory or would York City do all they could to raise his hopes only to smash them in his face like a custard pie full of broken glass?

There's only one way to find out. But whatever the outcome, showing such support for a team of losers, makes you more of a winner than those fly-by-nights who only support teams that usually win. Winning is for losers.

That's what I tell myself anyway and as York's most famous celebrity fan (what do you mean you've never heard of me?) I think that shows you just what losers and thus winners we all are.

Richard Herring

TEAM LINE-UP

Ingham

Purkiss   McGurk/Parslow   Sangaré/Graham   Meredith

Lawless/Smith   Mackin   Barrett   Ferrell/Carruthers

Brodie   Rankine/Gash

PROLOGUE

The stadium erupted around me. Thousands of ecstatic, bouncing fans celebrated the sweetest of last-minute winners. Every last one of them on their feet, revelling in the certainty of a victory they hadn't dared hope for: two minutes earlier, their team had been trailing. The August sun glinted back off their sunglasses; accentuated their bright yellow shirts. I remained seated, the only person in the stand to do so. I tried to block out the other spectators' mindless crowing. Full of the skewed optimism only an opening-day victory can bring, the joyous, gaudily-clad hordes danced and cheered all round me.

I wanted nothing to do with them. I closed my eyes and nursed my left foot, which was sore from having kicked the seat in front as hard as possible. It was the first time I had ever watched a match with the opposition fans. It will be the last.

I stood to leave, transferring as much of my weight as possible away from my damaged foot. Despite breaking into a Quasimodo limp, each tottering step triggered waves of pain. I shuffled up the steps to the back of the stand and hobbled out through the jubilant press room, cursing my own stupidity. I'd be needing that foot.

A year earlier I had set out from home for a spin on my bike. The aim had been to cycle from my flat in central London to Crawley, to watch my beloved York City play a football match. A leisurely ride on a beautiful summer morning. A quick dink over the Surrey Hills, a couple of pre-match pints with my fellow southern exiles, a win for York in the season's opening match and a train ride home. At least that had been the plan.

In reality I slept in, then compounded my late start by choosing to go off-road. I was trying to follow the Wandle Trail, a walking and cycle route which ostensibly follows the course of the River Wandle from Wandsworth to somewhere near Croydon. I figured I'd hug the Thames from my flat to the Wandle, then just sort of head for Gatwick when its trail ran out. This theory seemed sound within the confines of my head, but didn't stand up to closer scrutiny. The Wandle Trail printed in my A-Z bore no resemblance to its real life counterpart. It frequently petered out. Bits of it didn't exist. Signs led to dead ends in council estates; contradicted each other; pointed straight into the river. Somewhere south of Wandsworth, I got deeply lost. The clear blue sky bled to black.

Resurfacing a few hours later in Carshalton, I realised that I'd broken free of the boundaries of my A-Z. So I headed what I perceived to be due south on country lanes. I quickly got lost. It started pouring down. I got a puncture on the sharpest uphill stretch. I hadn't packed a repair kit. Or a coat. Or a map. I had to ask a man in a garage the way to the nearest train station. I'd done hardly twenty miles. The closest station turned out to be a mere couple of miles' walk away, uphill. I emerged in Crawley after a twenty-minute train ride; shame-faced, bedraggled and broken. At least I fitted in with the locals.

Some of the blame for this dreadful performance had to be shouldered by my bike: a battered old Specialized Hardrock bought for £35 when I first moved to the capital. It had served its purpose, dealing with the daily commute over South East London's potholed streets.

It hadn't dealt with it very admirably; in fact it had been woefully inadequate. Everything about the bike made cycling hard work. It was absolutely tiny, probably a child's bike. I'm not very tall at all but my knees would strike its handlebar grips on every upward pull. Its brake pads clamped steadfastly to its pitted, tar black rims at all times, except when they were applied. The tyres were bald and flat. Gear levers and chainset shared at best a passing acquaintance; its rear derailleur fishtailed around at will, selecting gears in an eenie-meenie-minie-mo fashion. Its handlebars and seat stem adopted a similarly whimsical approach to their supposed positions. It was the 1970s Holland of bikes: its constituent parts roamed around the frame in fluid movements, overlapping, getting caught out of position, returning languidly to their starting points when they fancied, if at all. Total bike.

Total shit though, it had to go. I eventually offloaded it to some poor bloke through the aptly named Freecycle, a website on which you offer things you no longer want for free. People express an interest in whatever you're giving away and then turn up at your door to collect it. The people who really want what you're offering tend to be very grateful, and a bit shy. Those who don't need what they've asked for tend to be rude and blasé: the stuff they collect invariably ends up on eBay. This guy genuinely wanted a bike and was pretty eager until he saw the minuscule abomination skulking in a corner. He was crestfallen, visibly pondering whether Freecycle etiquette allowed him to leave empty-handed, before reluctantly taking it. It was reoffered a couple of days later.

After its performance on the way to Crawley, I distanced myself from it on the train back to London, flinging it in the rack. The carriage was full of York fans. We had won 1-0 with a Craig Farrell shot midway through the second half. In off the post. Always a satisfying way to score. Full of hugely misplaced optimism for the season ahead, we travelled back to London in high spirits. One of our group, Dave, fished my bike out of the rack, riding it up and down the platform when the train made its frequent stops and up and down the corridors in between them. He could have chucked it on the tracks for all I cared.

Nevertheless, for all its flaws, this crappy little bike and the freedom it had given me had got me thinking. Completely ignoring my comprehensive failure to complete a short, straightforward journey, I started dreaming of what ifs. What if I cycled to *and* back from a York match? What if I talked a few mates into coming along for the ride? What if I went to a few games? What if I pedalled to and from every single match over the course of a whole season?

This last what if nagged away at me over the following months. I dug out the fixture list for the 2008-2009 season: it didn't seem *too* fanciful. Maybe even feasible.

I pored over maps, pawed at shiny new bikes. I made tentative enquiries to the club, to potential sponsors. I began to work out how best to package ten months' sporadic visits to my girlfriend. I started telling friends and family what I was thinking of doing. In short, I got excited.

At some point over the winter, I was surprised to find that this wishy-washy idea which had been swilling around my brain had begun to solidify. I heard myself being interviewed on the radio in March 2009 about my plans for the coming 2009-2010 season. I sounded like I knew what I was doing. I had ground rules. They were self-imposed, capricious and inconsistent, but ground rules is ground rules. Starting wherever the fixture list dictated, I would cycle to and from all forty-six of York City's Blue Square Premier league matches. My sole aim was to make it to the ground before kick-off. I decided to throw in FA Cup matches too. The memories of our heroic cup runs are fading fast: it would probably only mean one extra trip.

I ruled out watching the FA Trophy matches. We take the non-league knock-out competition too seriously and our progression inevitably wreaks havoc with a winter fixture list already disfigured beyond recognition by postponements. If I'd tried this in 2008-2009 I would have probably failed due to fixture congestion at the end of the season. I just wouldn't have coped with York to Weymouth in two days. Nor a match at Eastbourne followed a couple of days later by one in Altrincham. The pitches this far down the football food chain are a far cry from the blanketed, cosseted, undersoil-heated beauties which grace the top level. As a consequence, games are frequently called off over the winter months, often at the last minute. My final ground rule was to take the inevitable postponements in my stride; simply pedal on to the next match and worry about the rearranged one later.

Friends and family didn't seem too surprised. They asked no awkward questions. I think they saw it as the latest in a long line of daft endeavours. It was only in the telling of the story to people who didn't know me that the same question kept coming up: why?

The most truthful answers were the ones I couldn't give: at least not to strangers. Because I was thirty-two and I felt like life was passing me by; because since university I'd been living a passive, rudderless existence; because, like most of my peers, I was trapped in a responsibility-free world of perpetual adolescence; because I was getting fat and indolent; because it seemed like a bit of a lark. Mainly because it seemed like a bit of a lark.

There were other, more palatable reasons too; ones that were easier to say out loud. I'd lived away from York for the best part of fifteen years and I wanted to reconnect with the club that I used to follow so avidly. I wanted to raise money and awareness for the Alzheimer's Society. I wanted to write this book. I didn't want to become that guy staring into the bottom of his pint glass, thinking about this great idea he'd once had, and had never seen through.

So I handed in my notice at work. I gave up the lease on my flat in London; talked my Dad into letting me crash at his place in York. I bought myself a thrusting new steed: the staidly-named Kona Sutra. I somehow ended up buying two of them in a bleary-eyed 3am eBay frenzy. I had to import them from the United States. The customs charges and taxes ended up costing more than the bikes. I sold the powder blue one and kept the brash bright green one. It is a stunning machine, swift and solid. A breed apart from any other bike I've ever ridden. A different species from the shrivelled Specialized now condemned to Freecycle purgatory.

I looked forward to ten months without a job or a home. To thousands of lonely miles and hundreds of nights under canvas. To aching nuts and tattered buttocks. To pedalling through the night to make kick-off.

I steeled myself to watch my football team play forty-six matches in the worst professional league in the world. In comparison, the cycling would be easy.

AUGUST

Oxford.

A kindly fixture list had dictated that both the season and the challenge would start amidst dreaming spires and drunken scholars. Some of my more sadistic friends had insisted that I should have pedalled the 180 miles from York to Oxford prior to the opening match. This made absolutely no sense to me. Given that I was making up the rules, I ignored my mates. The whole point of this challenge was to go from match to match. I wouldn't be cycling back to York in between consecutive away games, I reasoned. In any case, I had just come back from two weeks' pre-season altitude training spent walking the *GR20* in Corsica with my girlfriend, Jola. We had only got back the day before the season started; I wouldn't have had time to make it to Oxford from York. No, I'd be starting at the Kassam Stadium, by happy coincidence a couple of miles from where Jola lived.

I'm still not entirely sure how I ended up sitting with the home fans. It's not something you really need to do as a York supporter; the demand for tickets is rarely high enough to force you to hide out in the other end. For one reason or another, I was the only one of our ragged, eclectic band of friends and football acquaintances who was going to the match. None of my York-based City-supporting mates were making the trip down. Most of the southern exiles were at Headingley to watch England's capitulation in the fourth Ashes test. I had spoken to Chris Williams, Oxford's incredibly helpful press officer, about storing my bike during the game. When I arrived, he showed me where to leave the bike and offered me a press pass. On a whim, I decided to watch the match from the press box. Then I bumped into Rupert Fryer, an Oxford fan who had interviewed me for the match day programme. We met for a pint before the game and watched the match together in the stand beneath the press box.

Rupert proved to be great company, but it was a mistake to sit with him. I should have taken my place with the rest of the red-clad fans in the away end. I had turned up to watch York home and away alone on several occasions over the years, and always enjoyed the solitude. You can focus more on the match: not that this is always a good thing. But it's much easier to be miserable amongst your own than when you're surrounded by the opposition's jubilant cries.

Before meeting Rupert, I loaded the Kona up with bulging rear panniers, a tent, roll mat, spare tyre, handlebar bag and water bottles. This was all the kit I'd have for the duration of the season. It didn't seem like an awful lot. The knowledge that it was just me and the bike for the following nine months filled me with giddy delight. I had no idea who I'd meet along the way, where I'd rest my head each night or how the season would take shape. All these unknowns excited me. I could do anything. Except pedal quickly. I hadn't done a fully-laden training run for a while and the lag from the extra thirty kilos came as quite a shock. I wobbled uncertainly off through Oxford's scruffy eastern fringes to the Kassam, their soulless corrugated horseshoe of a ground which had been plonked unceremoniously on a corner of an industrial estate. I'm sure Phileas Fogg had a more romantic, dignified and elegant send-off.

The Kassam Stadium lies a couple of miles out of the city on its south-eastern edge, backing onto the notorious Blackbird Leys estate. It is Firoz Kassam's poisoned legacy to Oxford United. Theirs is a tale familiar to clubs in this division and throughout the lower leagues: of broken promises, financial mismanagement and shady dealings.

Kassam bought the club for a pound in 1999. He quickly sold the dilapidated, idiosyncratic old Manor Ground to one of his own companies for £6m. Shortly afterwards he sold it on to developers, doubling its price along the way. The club then relocated to the current three-sided stadium, away from its Headington roots. A promised fourth stand has never materialised. Down among the non-league dead men, they don't really need it. If they manage to repeat their dizzy rises through the divisions of the 1960s and 1980s, perhaps then the stadium will be completed. Kassam sold the club on in 2006, but still owns and leases out the stadium which bears his name.

For a season-opener with half a new team, we played surprisingly well. Alex Lawless, a new signing from Forest Green, looked neat and tidy in midfield, rarely misplacing a pass and setting up a couple of chances. Half an hour in, he put our raw striker Richard Brodie clean through on goal. His initial shot clattered off the upright, but he reacted quickest, rifling in the rebound with his weaker right foot.

Brodie is a curious player who looks more like a ruddy-cheeked farmhand than a footballer. He runs around the pitch with a strange gait, arms kind of strapped to his side and head lolling about. This lulls opposition defenders into a false sense of security: he frequently takes advantage of their bewilderment to nip in and score. He runs and runs in his own inimitable style and gives his all, which is enough for most of the fans. The ones who give him a hard time for a ropey first touch or for missing a sitter will probably never be won over; their way to welcome a promising young player to the club is to hound them rather than to encourage. Bizarre behaviour when you think about it, to undermine your own club's players' confidence, but then some fans are happier being miserable.

Brodie had spent the first half of the previous season on loan at Barrow, until Martin Foyle was appointed York manager and he was quickly recalled. His nineteen goals the previous season had fired us to the FA Trophy final and, along with our 'keeper Ingham's saves, probably kept us in the division and in business. We would have struggled to survive in the Blue Square North as a full-time outfit. As a result, this bike ride would have been a leisurely potter round the North of England.

His goal here was enough to see us lead for most of the match, until a calamitous last minute. Oxford had been expected to win the match. They were favourites for the title and had added some shrewd acquisitions to an already solid side. We had six players making their debuts in the team, and had nearly been relegated last time out. We were doing well to push Oxford, and looked like waltzing off with all three points.

Until Parslow slipped to let in Matt Green, who lifted the ball over the onrushing Ingham and over the line. Well, somewhere near the line at least. It looked as if our left back, Meredith, had cleared it just in time but the goal stood. A point would be a decent return though from such a tricky match. Ingham must have been pondering just such an outcome when he raced uncharacteristically off his line to punch away a corner. He missed: Oxford's Creighton didn't. The big centre back side-footed home from the ensuing melee to spark pandemonium in the stands all round me. So this was the kind of season we were going to have.

I retrieved my bike and set off into the crowd, into the streets of Oxford and into the unknown. Well I got as far as Jola's anyway. We ate a simple meal together and said our reluctant goodbyes. There were a fair few tears. I'm sure one or two of them were hers.

A couple of miles later, I made the first of what would undoubtedly be many errors, dropping down off the road onto the canal towpath. I love cycling beside canals. You're immediately off the beaten track, you see herons and kingfishers and happy people waving at you – waving! – from their barges. They always seem so content with their lot, their pace of life so unruffled. Some of them do appear a little too cheerful, like they're part of some watery sect. But they soon disappear under a picturesque stone bridge and your attention is taken by spotting a water vole or swerving round a duck. Or best of all, pedalling along a logic-defying aqueduct, which invariably makes me feel like I'm gliding through an Escher painting.

It always takes me that beat too long to realise that canal towpaths aren't the best way to travel quickly; the idyllic surroundings override my capacity for logic. Don't be fooled by them looking more direct than the roads on the map. They are a dreadful way to travel if you want to make good time. They meander, adding miles and hours onto your route. Good wide stone paths peter out to boggy, rutted threads. Puncture hazards are everywhere. You're forever slowing down behind walkers or pulling over to let quicker cyclists through. The Oxford to Banbury stretch of the Oxford Canal is no exception. I was making pitiful progress. It would soon be dark. Somewhere in the fields north of Kidlington, I found my way back to the gently undulating Banbury road and followed it all the way to its end.

Once I'd broken free of the canal's clutches, I made good time. It was nearly dark when I got to Banbury so I asked around for a campsite. It was a busy, boisterous Saturday night, replicated in a thousand small towns across the country. Most of the locals were already drunk, and the sober ones had no idea where I might find a campsite. I fiddled around with my new lights for fifteen minutes or so, eventually admitting to myself that I had no idea how they worked. I could get the front one on fine. The rear one was supposed to plug in to the back of the front one and piggyback off it. As soon as it was plugged in it extinguished them both. Maybe it was meant to run off the helmet torch? Trying this also killed both lights. Why do I never try to work things out in advance? Waiting until they were first needed before finding out I couldn't operate them was pretty stupid. Annoyed at my habitual lack of preparation, I stuffed them in my handlebar bag. The front one turned itself back on.

I headed north out of town to find a quiet corner of a field. Well, I tried to. I went round the marketplace a few times, unable to find my way out. On my third lap, I saw another cyclist doing the same thing, but in the opposite direction. He was clearly lost, the amateur. I stalked him for a bit until I overheard him asking an elderly couple the way to the nearest campsite. I freewheeled over to listen to their reply. Armed with directions and hope, we were soon heading off together out of town. His lights worked pretty well.

Ian had set off that morning from Watford with the intention of getting to Warwick. He was on a three-day training tour in preparation for tackling Land's End to John O'Groats a few weeks later. He was hoping to complete the end-to-end ride in twelve days. He had bought himself a lovely new Thorn tourer which was well-balanced with front and rear panniers, and a swish new tent. He was better equipped for his trial run than I was for the nine long months ahead.

On the fourth drive-by, we found the campsite. The owner came out into the gloom to shepherd us in off the road. We put our tents up quickly. Ian calm and efficient with the help of his powerful front light; me in a dark, haphazard flail. A young girl from an adjacent tent kindly came and held her torch for me whilst I drove the pegs in. I'm not sure how she knew I needed help. Perhaps Ian had tipped her off. Tents in place, we wandered to the pub next door to swap excited plans.

In the morning we pedalled to the main road together before setting off in opposite directions. Ian pointed his bike south, I pointed mine north. And both of us heading home.

I spent a glorious couple of days zooming along sun-dappled B roads. I felt fit from the Corsican hike; the bike was sleek and gleaming, well oiled, smooth of gear and of wheel. This is what I'd signed up for: waking up of a morning with no idea where I'd end up that night; the astonishing drag of the panniers on an uphill stretch; the exhilaratingly giddy, unsafe speeds as they urged me back down.

The whole season stretched ahead of me in all its infinite possibilities. Would we finish fourteenth or seventeenth? How long before I got my first puncture? Before I missed my first match? Before I got on the train? The football was obviously going to be largely appalling, but in knowing this in advance, that concern could be set aside. I had a whole country to explore, and at the perfect pace. Cycling strikes an ideal balance of speed and flexibility. I could get my head down and make some serious miles in a day if needed. Or I could meander, double back, follow intriguing signs down woodland tracks. Nine months of this bliss were in store. I couldn't wait to plan out and set off on each new leg of the trip.

In this exultant mood I carved my way through the centre of England from Banbury to Derby, where my sister and her family live.

The following day, I battled through the North Derbyshire hills and struck out for York. I stopped to rest on a bench in the colliery town of Maltby. The old man at the other end of the bench struck up a conversation.

'You going far, lad?'

'Just to York.'

'Ah, you'll be there in no time. It's downhill to Donny from here, then it's flat as a pancake to York. We used to ride there and back in a morning. Long time ago now, though.'

'Blimey, you must have been quick.'

'I wasn't bad, but I had all on to keep up with my mate Tom.' He turned to me with a wistful gleam in his eye. 'He was lightning fast was Tom Simpson. I don't suppose you'll have heard of him?'

'Tommy Simpson. Really?! Of course I've heard of him. You used to ride with him?' I found it hard to contain my excitement that this unassuming old man used to be a riding partner of the greatest-ever British cyclist.

'Aye. He grew up just over the border in Nottinghamshire. We used to do club runs together. Lovely lad was Tom.'

His eyes had turned a little watery, his voice a little thin. I imagine we were both thinking of the same thing, but I didn't want to bring up his old friend's ignominious end. Simpson's death during the Tour de France in infernal conditions on Mont Ventoux has always struck me as a particularly horrific way to go. Climbing Ventoux's bare, dust-swept slopes in blistering heat and spurred on by a cocktail of alcohol, amphetamines and hubris, he cracked as he neared the summit, eventually falling unconscious into the road. Doctors were unable to revive him. He was twenty-nine.

I drank from my water bottle. My bench companion composed himself and then moved on to another local hero, the maverick cricketer Fred Trueman, who had been born and raised a stone's throw away in Stainton.

'If he'd been born a couple of miles south, he'd never have played for Yorkshire.'

He then segued into a complicated anecdote about a long-running feud with his neighbour over garden boundaries. At the end of it, this fascinating old man, whose name I never asked, got up to say goodbye and walked briskly off. Presumably to sort out his neighbour.

He was right about the route. Downhill all the way to Doncaster. Having only ever had bad experiences cycling through the town, I tried to pick my way round its western edge. Somewhere near Sprotborough I found a bike track that seemed to lead north. After a few hundred metres it narrowed to a point where it was no more than a rutted track dotted with brick-filled potholes. The panniers bumped and clattered against the rear forks, their reverberations numbing my arms and turning my beautiful Brooks saddle into a hostile no-go-zone. Somewhere near Scawthorpe I was spat gratefully back out onto tarmac. All this to avoid a town centre.

I'd only pedalled through Doncaster twice before. The first time was on a Land's End to John O'Groats trip, a few years before this trek. I had just polished off a healthy McDonald's breakfast and was struggling up a flyover bridge when I heard sirens. I hoisted the laden bike onto the pavement to make room, only for the police car to pull in just in front of me. Its occupant got out and made his way back to me.

'We've had a report of someone matching your description making off with a couple of laptops from a house nearby. I'm going to have to search your bags.'

I was wearing a bright yellow Alzheimer's Society T-shirt and a pair of black Lycra cycling shorts. My hair was at its most unruly; all windblown ginger corkscrews. Were they looking for a camp Mick Hucknall?

'Someone matching my description?' I believe I put my hands on my hips, accentuating the campness.

The policeman tipped back his cap and dabbed at his forehead with his index finger. He didn't believe I was the thief, but he was damn well going to see it through. 'That's what I've had radioed through. Can you open up the bags please?'

'Do you not think I would have a more effective getaway vehicle?'

He didn't ask a third time; he opened up the rear panniers, the only place I could have stored two laptops. He found a few crusty socks and a putrefying banana. After a minute's half-hearted rummaging we said our goodbyes and he sped off in search of more Huckalikes. The laptops were at the bottom, wrapped in a towel.

The second time I'd pedalled through Doncaster was to watch York, towards the end of the 2003-2004 season. Having not won since January, we were on the verge of sliding into the non-league abyss for the first time since our election to the Football League in 1929. Only a heroic win against champions-elect Doncaster Rovers could stave off relegation for another week. Then we'd just need to win the remaining two matches to complete a stunning escape. An escape which would surely begin at battered old Belle Vue.

We lost meekly, 3-1, dropping down into the fifth tier without a whimper. And we were still there six seasons later.

So you can see why I had no desire to add to my collection of Donny memories. Steering well clear of the murderous A19, I began to pick my way northwards through the villages that are strung out like bunting along the Vale of York's back roads. As I slowed down to round a corner in Norton, I heard an ominous crack from over my right shoulder. The back end of the bike seemed to have seized up. I dropped down the gears to make pedalling easier, but to no avail. The rear wheel would hardly turn. I ground to a halt in the car park of the School Boy pub. It wasn't the first time that I'd broken down outside a pub, but at least this time I could still stand.

I sprang off the bike and propped it against a table to inspect the damage. I'm in no way mechanically adept, but even I could tell that things weren't good. The little eyelet which had been holding the pannier rack in place had sheared off. As a result, the rear fork had lurched wildly to its left, straight into the gearset. I'd dislocated my bike.

Stupid bike. We'd been lifelong, inseparable mates for two whole days, and this is how it chose to repay me. I kicked its immobile back wheel and cried out in pain. Exactly the same contact point as the Kassam seat a mere two days before. All my enthusiasm and optimism for this whole escapade seemed to drain out of me. Boundless horizons had been narrowed in an instant to tunnel vision. I could hardly carry on with the bike snapped in two in such a crucial place. The fork, not Norton. The trip looked to be over before it had really begun. I did the only thing I could; went inside and ordered a pint.

The School Boy is a regular village pub, once owned by Doncaster Rovers legend Clarrie Jordan, whose 1946-1947 tally of forty-two league goals is still a club record. Its locals were congregated in the snug dark-curtained bar room. Within seconds of me sitting down, they'd ascertained what I was up to, where I'd come from, where I was trying to get to and why I'd stopped there. Before I knew it, a tiny old lady was leading me across the street to one of the village's two welders. The back door was one of those horse's stable affairs. Tony opened up the top half and rested his large glass of red wine on the bottom door while the old lady introduced us.

'Of course I'll help. I've got a bit of time before I pack. We're off up to the boat in Scotland tomorrow.'

He led me out to the garage and flicked on the light. I gasped. I thought I'd seen a ghost glimmering in the gloom.

'Is that a Silver Ghost?'

'Nay, lad. It's a 1928 Open Tourer. My oldest Roller that one.'

It transpired that Tony restores and hires out Rolls-Royces for a living. While he was explaining the ins and outs, he calmly set out all the welding equipment and manoeuvred me into a position where I could do least damage. The welder fizzed and crackled. With an admirably scant regard for health and safety, we set about patching up my bike, and the trip. I managed to hold the snapped fork together long enough for Tony to get a good join. At the third or fourth attempt he declared it up to scratch.

'That'll get you back to York at least.'

He looked me up and down as if he'd be surprised if I made it any further. While we were grappling with the bike, I'd explained to him that one of the toughest legs of the whole season was just around the corner. It consisted of three away matches in a row:

from York to Wrexham to Hayes in West London to Gateshead and back to York. In ten days. Before this, we had two home matches in a row. If the weld held, I would arrive in time for the Tuesday night match and would have to leave York after the second match, on the Sunday at the latest, in order to get to Wrexham in time. Four days to source a replacement frame. For a scarce bike. From a company which is notoriously difficult to contact. I could see where Tony was coming from.

He refused all offers of payment. I thanked him profusely.

'At least let me buy you a pint.'

He dismissed the idea with a shake of his white head and disappeared back into his house.

By the time I'd finished my pint, all my bags were inside, the bike was locked up and a fresh pint was in front of me. And a toad in the hole. I don't know how many of these things I organised myself, if any. The first forkful was halfway to my grateful mouth when Malcolm piped up from the bar.

'We're not letting you put your tent up in the park.'

'Oh, I...oh.'

'No. It's not right. We're not having it. Not right at all.' He paused to sup dramatically at his Stones. 'Not when you can use my spare room instead.'

Soft as anything us Yorkshire folk, once you get past the bluster.

The next morning, I zipped across the flatlands to York, fuelled by Malcolm's excellent breakfast. Despite the Kona being fully laden with panniers, the makeshift weld held. I got back in time to witness an exceedingly dull 0-0 draw with Rushden & Diamonds. Brodie's strike partner Michael Rankine had a first-half goal ruled out due to the ref missing an advantage. Rushden otherwise had the better of a very poor match. That's about all you need to know, and all I can remember.

When I eventually got through to the Kona suppliers, they confirmed my worst fears. No spare frames in the country in that size. They could get a replacement to me by the middle of the following week. I needed to be in Wrexham before then. I rang round all the Kona stockists I could find. Nothing doing. My old Dawes on which I'd cycled Land's End to John O'Groats was at my Dad's house in France. All my mates' bikes were either racers or mountain bikes: not a pannier rack in sight. I couldn't carry my tent and everything else on my back. I guess I could have set off without the bags and had them sent on, but I wanted to do the whole trip unaided. To cheer myself up, I pedalled to Bishopthorpe to see my Gran.

As always, she saw me coming long in advance. Her bungalow is at the end of a cul-de-sac and the living room window looks out on the rest of the street. As does Gran. Despite now having to walk with a frame, she was at the door before I was, all perm and dentures, greeting me with her usual 'Well, hello love!' She had recently celebrated her eighty-ninth birthday and was full of her habitual sparkle and gossip.

Her father had come from Alsace, her mother from Portrush. Half French, half Irish, she had always lived in York. She spent all her working life at Terry's chocolate factory, where she met my Grandad Fred. A tall, serious-looking man with deep-set eyes, he too worked at Terry's all his life. He was a noted amateur footballer and a keen York City fan. He wrote poetry, and taught himself how to paint. I remember him sharing with me his love of cricket, his constant chocolatey aroma and his dark blue Metro, which he drove quite badly. I wish I could remember more. He died in 1993, his mind ravaged by Alzheimer's.

Gran has lived alone in the bungalow ever since. We were pottering about in her back garden when my phone beeped. Twitter. I'd long been sceptical about signing up, but my old flatmate James – incredibly a Folkestone Invicta fan – had convinced me it would be a useful tool for spreading the word about my quest. I remained sceptical.

I opened the message. Another Tony, this one a journalist at *road.cc*, had read my narky tweet about the bike snapping. His reply was simple: a phone number and an offer of help.

In no time at all, he'd contacted Albert, a rep for British manufacturer Ridgeback, who rang me with an offer of a bike. Andy at Cycle Heaven in York would be happy to put it together for me; they'd have me on the road in no time. This was amazing. I could hare off round the country on a brand new machine and then send it back to Ridgeback when the Kona frame arrived. No need, said Albert, just auction it for the Alzheimer's Society at the end. The relief was immense. I really thought the whole trip had been coming crashing down round my ears. The Tonys, Albert and Andy had stunned me with their kindness. It's no exaggeration to say that they saved the trip from failure before it had even begun.

The new bike would be ready for me to pick up straight after the Saturday afternoon match at Bootham Crescent against Forest Green Rovers. Based in the hamlet of Forest Green, high up above the Cotswolds town of Nailsworth, FGR have punched consistently above their weight since they were promoted to the Conference in 1998. Three times they've finished one place above the relegation spots, and once in them, only to be reprieved by Northwich Victoria's demise. They've never really looked like making it into the Football League, but have become an established Conference side, indeed its longest-serving member. It's the sort of team we've become accustomed to losing to since we dropped down to this level. The general feeling amongst the fans before the match was that we would probably win this one. We would have to if we were serious about making any impact at all this season.

I met my Dad and a couple of mates for a pint before walking down to the ground. The crowd seemed pretty thin as we pushed through the turnstiles and made our way to the back of the David Longhurst stand, where the standing home fans congregate. This stand is the beating heart of the York City faithful, and is known by a few names. It was originally called the Shipton Street end, a name some of the fans still call it.

More often than not the name is simply shortened to 'the Shippo'. It was roofed and renamed in 1991 in memory of David Longhurst, who had tragically collapsed and died on the pitch the year before. It is a fitting memorial, and most of the York fans now refer to the terrace behind the goal as 'the Longhurst'.

There were noticeable gaps on its terraces, which but a few short years ago would have been regularly packed. The crowds have been dwindling for years, ever since we slipped out of the league. Today's was going to be particularly small. The attendance figure was hardly helped by the away following. Forest Green had brought eleven fans with them. Eleven. We counted. If they'd swapped with their on-pitch heroes, they could hardly have posed less of an attacking threat.

York were in the ascendancy for the whole of the first half, with Forest Green's 'keeper Burton repelling wave after wave of attacks. He kept up his defiant last-man stand until half-time, then simply carried on where he left off in the second half, making excellent saves from Neil Barrett, Brodie, and his former teammate Lawless. Just as it looked as if we were heading for a second consecutive goalless draw, Rankine was bundled over in the box and the referee pointed to the spot. He picked himself and the ball up and, after a half-hearted tug-of-war with strike partner Brodie, side-footed confidently in. Substitute Adam Smith added a second just before the end to secure the first three point haul of the season. It was the perfect send-off for one of the toughest legs of the whole trip.

When the fixtures had been first released back in July, the Gateshead away match had been benignly scheduled; an easy there-and-back from York, sandwiched between two home games. Unfortunately the fixture compilers had overlooked an athletics meet due to take place on the same day in the same stadium. It was tempting to imagine our players being snapped out of their customary lethargy by javelins raining down around them, but they spoilt the fun by switching the match. To a Tuesday night, three days after a trip to Hayes & Yeading, in West London. The sparkling new Ridgeback had ten days to get me from York to Wrexham to Hayes to Gateshead and back to York.

I picked it up straight after the match, just before Cycle Heaven closed. The next day, I pointed it towards North Wales and set off to chase my team all round Britain. I made it to Holmfirth without incident and pitched the tent. The hills in the Yorkshire Dales had barely troubled me; it had all seemed such a breeze. Within half an hour of leaving Holmfirth, I was crawling up a steep hill into the Pennines into something much stronger than a breeze. It was a fairly brutal road, all Pyrenean twists and turns. But the wind: oh, the wind! The hill alone was bad enough, with the panniers attempting all the time to drag me back down it. I was however making some progress, albeit slow. But when I rounded a hairpin and switched back on myself the wind hit me full in the face, bringing me to a standstill. A second, stronger gust actually sent me backwards. I laughed out loud. The next gust nearly knocked me off. I had just enough time to plant my foot firmly in the middle of a rabbit carcass. This time I managed to stifle the giggles.

When I eventually made it to the top, I stopped in the car park to shelter from the wind and to drink in the panoramic views of the reservoir-specked valley. A day-tripping couple were enjoying a cup of tea next to their car. I nodded and smiled, a suave man of the world. They didn't return the greeting. Perhaps they had overtaken me on the way up and were now met with a sweaty, red-faced, unshaven man scraping rabbit innards off his shoe, who they'd just seen laughing and swearing at the wind.

A glorious descent into Glossop and an afternoon picking my way across backroads got me to a campsite just east of Chester. I had a poke around the city in the morning before moving on to Wrexham. I'd never been before and was instantly charmed by its half-timbered arcades and almost intact sandstone City walls. Lovely place. Chester, obviously: Wrexham's awful.

I have to make a confession here. It's not about leaving the Holmfirth campsite without paying – I *did* knock on the door. I waited for five minutes but there was no answer. I tried to pay in Tarporley too, but there was nobody to be found when I left. No, it's not about minor camping indiscretions. It's much worse than that.

Quite often, when I'm all alone, I browse and post on a well-known football forum. I have a girlfriend, real-life friends and interests, yet still I spend some of my free time reading and typing stuff on the internet, laughing at and trying to entertain other anonymous men. I am a member of a forum. I am a forumer. I forum. There, I've said it. I feel a bit cleaner for having it out in the open. I'm sorry to have dirtied you in the process.

I had started a thread about this trip on the forum, which had generated a bit of interest. People had sponsored me, offered me advice, a pint at a match, even a bed for the night.

In Wrexham, I would meet a fellow forumer for the first time. The man who goes by the name of Myfanwy had suggested a campsite for me to stay at and a pub for us to meet in.

Catching sight of Myfanwy's Wrexham shirt, some York fans at the next table asked how we knew each other.

'We met on the internet.' Myfanwy's face went as red as his shirt.

He had the last laugh, though. We had a lot of possession, but most of it ineffectual. The half-time entertainment was more diverting: a procession of locals led out onto the pitch to sing out of tune in an attempt to win Wrex Factor.

Just before the hour, Wrexham's manager Dean Saunders introduced Manchester City loanee Adrian Cieślewicz. His lightning-quick runs immediately tore us apart. Wrexham took the lead within a couple of minutes of his introduction, Gareth Taylor nipping in to beat a shoddy offside trap and score with a neat glancing header. It was enough to win it. Four points from the first four games. Not exactly championship material.

Within a few early morning miles I was back over the border, barrelling along tiny Shropshire lanes flanked with hawthorn hedges and late-season cow parsley. The sun was shining brightly, the wind was at my back and my legs felt strong. I knew there would be much trickier times to come on the trip but for the moment, pedalling was pure pleasure. As I made for Shrewsbury, a long-forgotten song lodged itself in my head. A song at odds with the bucolic beauty whistling past my ears:

> Oh Shrewsburyshire (oh Shrewsburyshire),
> Is full of shit (is full of shit),
> Oh Shrewsburyshire is full of shit,
> It's full of shit, shit and more shit,
> Oh Shrewsburyshire is full of shit.

This snippet of lyrical genius is reproduced with the kind permission of the York City away crowd, February 1993. My friend Will and I had travelled down on the supporters' coach from York to Shrewsbury for a Barclays League Division Three match. Despite being in the middle of a run which would bring one win in thirteen attempts, we were still very much in with a shout of promotion. At seventeen we had the time and, somehow, the money to get to most matches that season.

I can't recall much of the game at Gay Meadow other than Canham's lobbed equaliser, the above geographically inept chant and our left back Wayne 'Ginner' Hall hitting his trademark corkscrews over the Riverside stand into the Severn. There used to be a man who sat in a coracle and, later, an inflatable dinghy throughout Shrewsbury's matches, to fish stray balls out of the river. Ginner's wayward clearances kept him busy that day.

It was a great time to be following City. Under John Ward, York had flown out of the traps, winning eight of the first nine matches. I can still recall the full line-up, which barring an occasional switch at centre back, was pretty much the same every week:

	Kiely		
McMillan	Stancliffe	Warburton/Atkin	Hall
McCarthy	Pepper	Swann	Blackstone
	Barnes	Borthwick	

Ward left for Bristol Rovers in March, but his departure didn't derail the promotion push. Alan Little took over and guided us to a strong fourth-place finish, just outside the automatic promotion spots.

Ginner took the decisive penalty in the play-off shoot-out at Wembley to secure promotion. As he ran up to strike it, you could almost hear people praying *'keep it down'*. He took heed, calmly pea-rolling it into the bottom corner to spark pandemonium in the York end.

Sixteen years later, Shrewsbury was shimmering in the early afternoon sun. It's a handsome town from the Severn up; all winding cobbled streets and half-timbered houses. I sunned myself outside a riverside pub, wishing I had longer to spend there.

But I had to keep going. It was Wednesday afternoon and I had to be in London for the Hayes & Yeading match on Saturday. This wasn't too onerous a task: about seventy miles a day. A mere taster for what was to come after the match in London: a three-and-a-bit day, 300-mile dash to Newcastle. With this in mind, I reluctantly pushed on.

A few hours later, I was flying down a steep hill into Bridgnorth. Halfway down, I was jeered at by some leering, beeping fuckwits. I was only a few hundred miles into the trip and sick to death already of idiots like this driving too close, chucking stuff at me, shouting 'Wanker!' as they passed. Why do so many drivers react to cyclists like this? They can't *all* know me.

I stopped for a breather on the equally steep hill back out of town. The car the people had shouted from overtook me and stopped in the same lay-by. It's occupants opened the boot, took out a beer, gave it to me, put my panniers in the boot, handed me another beer to replace the one I'd just drained and told me there'd be plenty more where that came from in thirteen miles' time. And a curry. And my bed was made. Helen and Gary: they're not fuckwits at all, and I've never seen them leer. A bit sharp on the horn perhaps, but they'd not heard from me since I'd left Shrewsbury and were slightly concerned, so they'd driven out to find me. It's incredible how much difference riding without panniers made. Those thirteen unladen miles were quite hilly, but some of the easiest of the whole trip.

Helen and I had been flatmates at University. We had also worked together in a bingo hall, filling the gaps in our split shifts with red wine. After we'd polished off her excellent curry, we shared a bottle or two for old times' sake and reminisced long into the night.

After a brief stay in Oxford I battled over the surprisingly abrupt Chilterns and into London for the Hayes & Yeading match. The first of several trips to the capital, and the first of many stays at Will's flat in Ealing.

We set off to walk the few miles to Hayes & Yeading's Church Road ground on the morning of the match: Will, his brother Stu, me and the bike; but it quickly became apparent that Will's estimate of an hour's wander had been hopelessly optimistic. So they hopped on a bus and I hopped on my bike. A mile or so from the ground, I caught up with a cyclist in a York shirt, another Will, who was cycling to Church Road and back from Romford. He told me that he tries to pedal to at least one match each season. The security man let us both put our bikes in a shed inside the ground. I don't think either of us paid to get in.

Inside the ground I met Ray, Hayes & Yeading's photographer. He gave me a potted history of the club.

'There was 18,000 here once in 1951 for an amateur cup match. People were pouring over that fence there. Course it was just Hayes in them days.'

The two clubs had only merged in 2007, securing promotion to the Conference National in their second season. They had both been members of the Conference South at the time, but struggled to attract many supporters due to their proximity; both clubs played in Hayes.

'You expecting many in today?' It was close to kick-off and the crowd was still very sparse. We usually take a good number of away fans for this level, especially in London, as the southern exiles turn out in force. Not today though; the indifferent start to the season had dented the numbers.

'Well we had to redo the programme once we got promoted. Could hardly hand a pamphlet out at this level, could we? We have to do a print run of 500. We need to sell 350 to break even. I think we'll just about do it today.' The crowd was later announced as 606. That's a hearty take-up rate if they're going to break even.

The first half was the kind of dull, aimless affair that makes up the bulk of a season. Will – not the cycling one - took it upon himself to enliven things. Just before half-time the ball trickled out for a throw-in, directly in front of where we were standing. Will reached down over the low wall and threw the ball back to Purkiss to save a few seconds. His legs flicked up in the air with the effort. It looked for a moment that he'd be able to correct himself, but eventually momentum took over and he tumbled head first in a surprisingly graceful arc, over the wall onto the side of the pitch.

He popped immediately back up, grinning widely at those jeering him from the stands. He was oblivious to the blood pouring from a nasty cut above his eye. I was due on the pitch at half-time, so took him with me to get patched up. The Hayes & Yeading supporters' club had very kindly offered a cheque for the Alzheimer's Society and a signed shirt to raffle at the end of the season. They had wheeled me and the bike out on to the pitch at half-time to make the presentation. As I wandered back down the touchline afterwards, several Hayes & Yeading fans, including the chairman, put more money into the pot. Meanwhile, Will was getting patched up in the physio room and realised he could hear people talking about him from the next room.

'Did you see that silly bugger land on the pitch?'

'Yeah, what did he think he was playing at?'

'Oi, that was me!' Will popped his head out into the tunnel to see the ref and linesman laughing their heads off at him. The Hayes & Yeading player Justin Cochrane holds a special place in his affections for breaking up the party and making sure that he was all right.

Early in the second half, Ingham rushed (slightly less uncharacteristically this time) off his line and rashly felled Daly, who scored the resultant penalty. Ingham was very fortunate not to be sent off. York huffed and puffed for the rest of the match. Hayes & Yeading should have put the result beyond doubt, but hit the woodwork a couple of times. Richard Pacquette came off the bench to nod in a hugely undeserved equaliser. Will's celebrations were more muted than usual. Five points from the opening five games. It was going to be a long old season.

I set off straight after the match, needing to be in Newcastle in a little over three days' time. My target for the evening was to stay with my mate John in Cambridge. I would have to cycle into the night to make it that far, but fortunately John would be on a night out in the middle of town. It took quite a while to negotiate West and North London's myriad streets, and it was starting to get dark by the time I trundled past Barnet's Underhill ground.

I'd worked out how to use the lights by this point and they were incredibly bright; as bright as any of the cars coming towards me on the Hertfordshire lanes. I had to ride with the clear lenses in my sunglasses to fend off incoming moths. I was an immediate convert to night riding. The roads were quiet, the air still; this was a wonderful way to travel. I got to Cambridge about 1am. John was still in the town centre, coming to the end of a long night's drinking session with a couple of workmates.

Despite being a Huddersfield Town fan, John has a lot of decent human qualities. We met on the first day at University, bonding over our love of crap football teams – York and Huddersfield were in the same league at the time – and realising that we were doing the same course. We had since lived together in Scotland and France and have always kept in close contact. In the fifteen years we've known each other, John's ability to hold his drink hasn't increased one iota. He's always been a knockabout, loved-up drunk and this night was no different.

He didn't love me quite as much in the morning when I woke him up to let me out. I had some serious miles to do; an early start was imperative. I decided to keep as far to the east as possible to let the very timely southerly wind speed me across the flatlands of the Fens. I was in Peterborough in no time. It is not the best-looking city in the world, but it proved to be one of the best on the whole trip for cycling. It seems to have been built on a strict concrete-monstrosity-to-cycle-path ratio. Well-signposted off-road routes criss-cross the city. Barring the cathedral, Peterborough is awful to look at but a real pleasure to pedal through.

I was in Lincoln before I encountered a hill worthy of the name. I'd already done about 100 miles - more than any other day on the trip so far, but I still felt good. It was apparent that I'd come a bit *too* far east. I'd have to go over the Humber Bridge and up the east coast of Yorkshire from here. It didn't matter. That's what the trip was all about – making it up as I went along and making already difficult situations even tougher. I stopped at a campsite north of Lincoln. The odometer read 117 miles for the day, the most I'd ever pedalled in one day by some considerable distance. And I had to do it all again when I woke up.

It was pretty late by the time I'd got my tent up, but the campsite bar was still open. I sat outside with the owner, who explained to me his unique licensing system. I could have as many beers as I wanted, but I couldn't pay for them. The bar was unlicensed. The police made frequent visits, so to circumvent their awkward questions he gave the beer away. All the guests were, however, encouraged to make a donation for drinks consumed. The long day in the saddle had been pretty thirsty work. The owner poured me four free pints, carefully covering the pump handle with a sheet each time. I donated a tenner for the upkeep of his fine bar.

Coming out of Brigg the next morning, I caught up with an old guy on an equally old Mercian tourer which seemed to be held together with bar tape and string. Stan was heading off for the Lake District on his decrepit machine, stopping in youth hostels along the way. He showed me the best way to the Humber Bridge and pedalled serenely away.

I carried on up and over the bridge, through Beverley and Driffield, and struck out for the coast. Coming down Caxton Hill, I hit forty-two mph. It was an exhilarating, frightening descent. The panniers were buffeting around in the wind and it took all of my strength and concentration to hold the handlebars straight. It would be the quickest I'd go on the whole trip.

The old Scarborough to Whitby railway line is now an energy-sapping cinder track. I was done for by the time I got to the end, and it was getting dark. Whitby was playing host to one of its many festivals, so there was nowhere to stay. I pedalled wearily on, up into the moors, with the intention of flinging my tent up in a field in the middle of nowhere. At the top of a hill I spotted another B&B, the Swallow's Nest. There was no room there either, but Sue offered a corner of the garden for my tent. While I was putting it up she came back out with tea and sandwiches, accompanied by her husband Keith. They invited me in for more tea and insisted on making me a pack-up for the morning.

Keith asked me what I was up to, so I gave him the now usual spiel about the trip. He told me that he'd been watching Sheffield Wednesday since the 1950s.

'Who's the best player you've seen in all that time?'

He didn't pause to think. 'Tom Finney. The man could do anything. I remember watching him play for Preston at Hillsborough towards the end of his career. Ran the show. He bagged himself a hat-trick. Ran the length of the pitch for his third. Our lads couldn't get near him. Couldn't touch him.' Keith shook his head in undiminished disbelief.

I made a mental note to ask Sir Tom if he remembered this match; I was due to meet him in a couple of weeks' time.

I retired to bed knackered but once more staggered by strangers' hospitality and kindness. It was Monday night; I'd knocked off 285 increasingly hilly miles since full-time on Saturday. One more seventy-mile push to Newcastle and I would make it.

An amazing morning spent flitting across the tops of the North York Moors, then a skip up the coast from Guisborough to Newcastle, delivered me to Gateshead well before kick-off and in good humour. Even an unlikely downpour from a clear blue sky couldn't dampen my spirits.

Gateshead's International Stadium incorporates all the worst elements you could possibly wish for in a football ground: stands situated miles away from the pitch to accommodate a running track; banks and banks of empty seats; uncovered stands from which crowd noise dissipates into the cold north air. Any attempts at creating an atmosphere are short-lived; only bitter rain echoes back.

A decent York following did its best to generate some noise from the clouds. Gateshead had the better of the first half, taking the lead just before the break with a screamer of a shot from Alex Francis. He was helped by our entire defence backing off and inviting him to shoot, but he made the most of the opportunity, thrashing it in from well outside the area.

In the second half, the match degenerated into the kind of Keystone Cops farce which comes along quite often at this level. An excellently created and executed goal by Brodie cancelled out Gateshead's opener, but it was followed a minute later by Pacquette's dismissal for retaliation. Our manager Martin Foyle was sent to the stands for his reaction to the decision. Djoumin Sangaré came on for an erratic cameo debut full of beautifully-timed tackles, a booking for a less well-timed one and all kinds of languid genius from the centre of defence. A cult hero in the making. I sponsored his boots the next day.

As so often happens, we were stung into action by the dismissal and conjured up a winner eight minutes from time. Michael Gash opened his account for the club with an emphatic header from the tireless Ferrell's perfect cross, which had probably rolled out of play.

An unjust victory from nowhere, like rain from a cloudless sky.

I stayed overnight with my cousins Gavin and Adam, who rode out with me in the morning. Adam is younger and much fitter than me. He's also unfailingly polite and pretended not to mind that we were travelling at half his usual speed. He left me on a bike track close to the city centre and I set off home for the final leg of this mini Tour of Britain. We'd had a late start, so I stopped overnight in Darlington, pootling the last few miles back to York the next day. As I passed Rowntree's factory on the way into the city, I glanced down at the odometer in time to see it click round to 1,000 miles.

I checked my emails when I got back to Dad's flat. In amongst them was one from Ian, of Banbury campsite fame. He had made a fantastic start to his end-to-end attempt, making it all the way from Land's End to Kendal in the first week. As he reached the top of Shap Fell, he had felt something in his knee twang. Realising it was quite serious, he coasted down the other side to the nearest village for help. Here, he was directed to the nearest hospital in Penrith, nine hilly miles away. Wanting to continue the trip at all costs, he pedalled there, knee searing in pain with every rotation. The doctor put an end to any fanciful notions Ian may have had of finishing the trip. He had torn a tendon in his knee and would need crutches and rest.

Having witnessed Ian's infectious enthusiasm at first hand, I was really sorry he couldn't finish his trip, and his misfortune made me realise that I was only ever one strain, twist or fall away from having to abandon mine. With the first 1,000 miles done, I was probably only a tenth of the way through it. I hoped my body would be tough enough to see the rest out.

Back at Bootham Crescent, one of our many bogey teams lay in wait. Histon are a big strong physical side, the likes of which always cause us problems. In fact we'd never beaten the Cambridgeshire minnows before.

From the first whistle, you could sense this meeting would be different. A first half of near-constant York pressure should have yielded more than just the one goal, a deftly-steered Brodie header from a Ben Purkiss cross. On the hour, Brodie was swept off his feet in the box only for Adam Smith to make the most of the referee's excellent advantage by firing home from twelve yards. A few minutes after that, Brodie was once more knocked to the ground, this time quite clearly well outside the box. The ref pointed immediately to the spot. Brodie converted low and hard to the 'keeper's right. A late consolation for Histon courtesy of Ingham's lapse in concentration could hardly take the gloss off an excellent attacking display. A 3-1 victory to close out the month. Back-to-back wins had elicited that most dangerous of feelings: hope.

SEPTEMBER

'We're going to have to stop in a minute.'

'You all right, mate?'

'I'm fine. I just need to stop for a sec, that's all.'

'Fine, as long as you're OK.' *He needs a piss.*

'Let's just pull over here for a bit.' He indicated a narrow road running parallel with the A59, along which we were travelling. 'I want to show you the spot where a cow ate my Brooks saddle. And I could do with a wee.'

The wave of déjà vu almost knocked me off my bike. I even knew what my lame joke reply would be before I said it.

'Isn't that cannibalism?'

'Very funny. Unless you have to stand up all the way home.'

Dad had told me this story so many times before, but I had never been able to place the bridge in my mind. This was the first interactive version.

We duly stopped by the river to inspect the spot where the bovine indiscretion had occurred. An eleven-year-old Dad had pedalled out to Skip Bridge to do a spot of peaceful fishing. A curious cow spotted his unattended bike and began to attack the saddle, eating a big chunk of it and digesting it in its four stomachs while Dad fished on oblivious. If grudge-bearing were to be introduced to the Olympics, Dad would be nailed-on for a gold medal. He was still irked by a petty crime committed by a long-dead cow half a century ago.

Skip Bridge is only a few miles west of York, and we were already on the third or fourth unscheduled toilet break. Dad was accompanying me some of the way to Barrow-in-Furness. We were aiming for his old rugby teammate's place in the Yorkshire Dales. We had rebuilt the Kona together with the replacement frame they had supplied and I was now back on the green machine, in the hope that the previous problem was a one-off rather than a design fault. Dad was riding the Ridgeback, which he loved.

'I'm enjoying it you know, mate.'

'The cycling?'

'No, not really. The football. We seem to have the makings of a team this year.'

Dad has been going to Bootham Crescent on and off since the 1960s. He followed them a lot as a youngster, before girls and work intervened. Since his retirement he had once again started watching an occasional match. I can't blame my life-long affliction on him: I started watching York during one of his fallow periods of support. In fact in recent years it had been me dragging him along to Boxing Day matches and one-off games when I'd been in town. What I was doing this season had seemed to pique his interest: he'd been to all the home matches so far. I'd been enjoying his unexpected company. It was nice to grab a pint with him and my mates beforehand, and his grumbling and moaning at the players' ineptitude had so far remained just the right side of amusing. The best thing about his negative outbursts was that they usually heralded a York goal.

He was right about the team starting to come together after the sluggish start. Another physical side, Crawley Town, had been seen off the day before at the Crescent.

In his understated fashion, Dad was impressed. 'That dark-haired lad in the middle can play a bit, can't he?'

'Lawless?'

'Aye, that's the one. He's a *footballer*.'

'Well yes, you'd hope so. I think that's why we're paying him.'

'You know what I mean, clever arse. He plays with his head up, makes things tick. A real *footballer*.'

York have had their fair share of Ali Diaesque non-footballers over the years, but Alex Lawless certainly wasn't one of them. He had been a revelation so far, by far my favourite signing of the summer.

The leader of the vicious "droogs" gang in *A Clockwork Orange* had been named Alex by Anthony Burgess as a play on words; a-lex means outside the law in Latin. Knowing this made me like our new midfielder even more: who wouldn't want a Lawless Lawless marauding around the centre of the park in their colours? Fortunately he isn't as malicious as Burgess' Alex; although prone to mis-timing the occasional tackle, he isn't a particularly nasty player. But oh my brothers he could viddy passes his droogs could not, and was not afraid to grab a game by the yarbles.

Against Crawley, he had started in the centre of midfield instead of out on the right where he'd been recently marooned. Revelling in the extra responsibility, he had been imperious, creating several chances in the opening ten minutes. We scored two of them. Brodie's persistence won another penalty, which he converted low and hard to the 'keeper's right. A few minutes later he flicked on a Meredith throw in to his strike partner Gash, who swivelled and crashed home from eight yards. No further goals were added, but this did not detract from an utterly dominant display. Gash and Brodie had only been paired together for the last three matches, but they'd scored six between them and we'd won them all.

Towards the end of the match, Andy Ferrell earned a huge cheer for a pleasingly despicable challenge on Simon Rusk, adding to his already impressive yellow card collection in the process. Before moving to Crawley, Rusk had 'played' for York, his lacklustre 2008-2009 displays epitomising the lack of desire and application which saw us slide perilously close to the Blue Square North and probable oblivion. In his penultimate appearance he was sent off for a cowardly stamp at Grays Athletic. Surprisingly recalled for the FA Trophy final, he spent most of the match in hands-on-hips bewilderment in the Wembley centre circle as Stevenage passed round him on their way to an easy victory.

With the Crawley match sufficiently dissected, Dad and I found ourselves in Ripon for lunch. We had a quick bite to eat in the shadow of Ripon's magnificent cathedral, then headed for the real place of worship in Masham.

Paul Theakston founded the Black Sheep brewery in 1992. Disillusioned with Scottish & Newcastle's protracted takeover of the long-running family brewing business, T&R Theakston, he decided to set up on his own instead. His brewery is now a rollicking success, and his excellent beers are widely available throughout the UK and beyond. But the best place to sample them is at source. We sat down at the bar in the brewery's visitor centre and tucked into the freshest of fresh pints.

We wobbled off into Wensleydale, down tiny lanes edged with dry stone walls that bound beautiful sheep-speckled fields. Wensleydale is the only one of the Dales not named after its river. The River Ure winds through Upper and Lower Wensleydale before changing its name near Boroughbridge and flowing through York and out to the North Sea as the River Ouse. At Aysgarth, the Ure tumbles down a short but majestic shallow-stepped limestone staircase. It seems like a pretty leisurely, harmless incline. Until you start cycling up the adjacent road. Perhaps it was the third pint of Black Sheep holding us back, but it was a real struggle. Dad toiled even more than I did, although he shouldn't by rights have been cycling at all.

In 2006, a car crash in France had left him in a coma for a month. He broke most of the bones in his body. His spine, skull and legs were the worst affected; he was very fortunate not to lose his right foot. His rehabilitation has been a long, slow process. This ride was another milestone on the way to recovery. Dad would return to York the next day, but promised to join me for a week-long bickering session later in the season.

We stopped for the night at his mate Graham's, high up in the hills near Hawes. A tiny, dead end forest lane leads to the secluded hamlet, which looks out over the dale. The Pennine Way passes by not far from their back door. Red squirrels dart around in the front garden. It's difficult to imagine a more idyllic retirement spot.

I made it to Hawkshead the next night, sweeping through stunning Dentdale to Sedbergh and crossing into Cumbria in the process. A toil of a climb towards Kendal was rewarded with a panoramic view of the town and the Lake District's fells beyond.

I fancied I could see the sea, and thought I might be able to pick out Barrow, before realising that the vast expanse of blue was probably Windermere. All alone at the top of the hill, I blushed.

When I eventually got to the lake, I took the ferry across and pedalled alongside Esthwaite Water until I got to Hawkshead, its cluster of whitewashed cottages giving off an inviting glow in the gathering gloom. After a night at the town's campsite I pedalled to Barrow. It was still morning when I got there; there were hours and hours to spare before kick-off.

'Where are you off to, mate?' The scruffy-looking bloke outside the tourist information centre was taking a bit too much interest in my bike.

'Here. I'm going to Holker Street tonight for the match. Is there much to do round here?'

'Not really, mate. It's not the sort of place people come to really.'

Quite. Barrow is a grim-looking industrial town at the end of a peninsula, with a National Park on its doorstep. It's not surprising it gets overlooked. For want of distraction, I went to the ground.

General Manager Martin kindly let me shelter in the bar above the away terrace, overlooking the pitch. A squally wind lashed rain against the bar windows. I had a detour to do on the way back to York and needed to set off into that filthy weather after the match in order to get a head start.

The match itself was a non-event played in tricky conditions due to the swirling wind and rain. Given its position out on a limb, I imagine this is a frequent occurrence at Holker Street. Barrow seemed keen to avoid a repeat of their previous result, a 6-1 thrashing by Rushden, and were certainly more accustomed to playing in the gale, even managing to occasionally keep the ball on the deck. They had the better of the match, but we had the better of the chances; Brodie missed a sitter of a diving header and Gash hit the bar with a lob. A fourth win on the bounce never really looked like coming and the game finished goalless.

I was traipsing back down the stairs from the bar after the match when I was stopped in my tracks by a hearty slap on the back. I turned round and was greeted by a jovial-looking bloke with a white beard and glasses who I'd never seen in my life before.

'Hello Simon, it's your Uncle Graham.'

'Really? You look nothing like him.' I do have an Uncle Graham, who's also a York fan.

'I know, he's shorter and fatter than me.' He had me on the back foot now. I stuck out a hand in confusion.

'Graham Bradbury.'

In a dark recess of my dusty mind, a tiny light bulb flickered. 'Did you used to play footy with my Dad?'

'Certainly did. At Bish. I know your Mum from back then too. She drove me to hospital when I broke my leg. She still remembers what I said to the doctor after they'd put the cast on – "Will I be able to swim, doc?" "Course you can, once it's healed" "Well that's great news, 'cos I couldn't before." Always remembers that, does your Mum.'

Another hearty slap on the back and we went our separate ways: Graham to drive back to York, whilst I pedalled off into the wind, rain and dark with only a 0-0 draw to warm the soul. If I could somehow have harnessed some of Graham's energy, I would have made short work of the lonely miles.

I woke to a sound I hadn't heard for weeks. My alarm: shrill and insistent, piercing the calm of the tent. On the fourth snooze cycle I remembered why I'd set the thing so early; I had to get from wherever I was in the Lake District to Preston for 2pm.

I unzipped the tent, rolled out of my sleeping bag, out of the tent and nearly into the stream below. Scrabbling for purchase on the steep dewy bank, I wondered what had possessed me to pitch the tent so close to the water. I got my answer by way of a squelch. The sort of squelch made only by bare foot on cowpat. The same foot that had been up to the ankle in rabbit guts a couple of weeks before. At least that time it had been clothed.

I packed the tent in a rage-fuelled record time, pausing only to note that my head had been precisely over another pat all night. Once the tent was stuffed into its sleeve, I hauled it, the bike and the panniers over a stile onto the hump-backed bridge above.

A driveway gave out onto the road just to the right of the bridge. A freshly-delivered crate of milk was winking at me from atop the drive's dry stone wall. Figuring that karma had got its retaliation in first, I nicked a pint and dropped back over the stile to the meadow below. Tip-toeing back through the cowpat minefield, I realised that I had inadvertently chosen an idyllic campsite.

A few short hours before, I had pedalled away from Barrow and had ended up ten miles or so north of Ulverston, in the middle of nowhere. After some undignified groping about in the dark, I slept on what turned out to be a sheep-nibbled meadow in the lee of an ancient stone bridge which arched over a glass-clear stream.

Perching on the bank with my feet dangling in the stream, I laughed out loud at how bloody lucky I was to be doing what I was doing.

I washed the cow shit off my foot, the smell of it out of my hair and drank my stolen milk. Reuniting the empty bottle with its full crate-mates, I set off through the early morning haze to meet a Knight of the Realm.

An old school friend had arranged for me to meet Sir Tom Finney. At school, Richard had been a brilliant goalkeeper and golfer, and also a committed York fan. He was now a vicar in Preston. The now Reverend Bunday had been chatting to Preston North End's chaplain about all manner of things, including my trip and the charity I was raising money for along the way. North End's chaplain suggested Richard contacted Sir Tom, a supporter of the Alzheimer's Society, with a view to organising a meet-up.

So he did. The meeting had been set up before the fixture list had been finalised, so it was pure luck that I was even anywhere near Preston on the designated day. As it was, I still had sixty-odd miles to cover before 2pm. I only remember stopping twice: once for breakfast in Lancaster and once to sick up the pilfered milk.

We had been due to meet at Deepdale, the famous old ground where Finney had spent his entire career. Sir Tom was fresh out of hospital and still a little woozy, but instead of calling off our meeting he insisted it went ahead at his house instead. It turned out to be quite a surreal experience. Just before the allocated time I was milling around on Sir Tom Finney's driveway with the Reverend Bunday, a woman representing the church who had kindly collected for the charity, an undertaker who had also donated, a photographer and a journalist. It must have looked like a scene from a really bad sitcom pilot. In fact it's probably already in pre-production for BBC3.

We had been tipped off to wait for one of Sir Tom's friends before going in. Dead on two o' clock, a sprightly man bounded up the drive with a foil-covered plate in his hand.

'Afternoon, I'm George. Just bringing Tom a bite to eat. I'll just make sure he's feeling all right, I'll be back in a minute.'

Before he had time to come back out, another man arrived and shook hands all round.

'I'm Tommy. Just popped round to see Tom. He's doing well, but the drugs have knocked him sideways a bit.'

I later found out that the two men were George Ross and Tommy Thompson, who had played in the same Preston team as Sir Tom. Tommy was an England international who had scored thirty-four times in the 1957-1958 season, the one in which Finney tore Keith's Sheffield Wednesday apart.

They didn't say as much but were obviously anxious to avoid Sir Tom being overwhelmed by a group of people descending on him at home when he was just out of hospital. For all his media experience and comfort in the limelight, he was still a convalescing old man. It was great to see his old teammates looking out for him after all these years. They led us into his home, an unassuming little bungalow the likes of which you see all over the country. In fact, it was pretty much an exact replica of my Gran's in Bishopthorpe. Same bay window overlooking the drive; same small, neat garden; same framed England shirts and photos of her in action at Deepdale and Wembley all over the walls.

Sir Tom was welcoming, affable and kind. He made time to speak to every single one of the strangers who'd congregated in his front room. The photographer made him hold my York scarf aloft in a mock signing session. If our current strikers keep performing as they did at Barrow, he may well get a run-out.

He was a bit distant, a little shaky, his memory unreliable. All that can be put down to his recent hospital trip and whatever drugs he'd been on whilst he was in there.

I hoped in the context of why we were there that it was nothing more.

Once we got talking about football he was on firmer ground. I asked about the match that Keith so vividly remembered.

'Yes. I remember that one. The team played well that day.'

No mention of his own heroics, even when I pushed him on it. This was in line with everything I'd heard about Sir Tom beforehand. Humble and friendly: a gentleman. A true legend of football, undervalued as that word has become by being attributed to every two-bit mercenary who passes through a club. The game will never see his likes again.

Back at the vicarage the Reverend Bunday and I sank a few beers whilst watching England demolish Croatia in the World Cup qualifier.

In the morning I decided to go to Deepdale to have a mooch round the National Football Museum. I got almost immediately lost, so stopped a guy in an England cricket top for directions. His accent threw me.

'Aye, just go through this park till ye get tae the Stanley Matthews statue, ye cannae go wrang.'

'Tom Finney?'

'Whatever.'

Sir Tom wouldn't have minded, I'm sure.

I didn't stay long in the museum. I'd left the bike at the front desk and the people behind it were unreassuringly non-committal as to whether it would still be there on my return. It was a bloody nuisance sometimes. It was all right at night when I could drag the panniers inside the tent and lock the bike outside, but if I left it anywhere in the daytime I just had to trust people not to take it, bags and all. Which either led to rushed visits or to dragging the cumbersome thing around with me. I could hardly do the latter in the National Football Museum so I had to hope for the best. I sped around, trying to take in as much as I could but all I can recall is a blur of shirts behind glass and brown leather balls.

Before heading back to York for the Cambridge match, I made another detour down to Chorley to say thanks to one of my sponsors, Paul Elliot, who'd supplied me with my helmet. I got there to find that it was his day off. I didn't begrudge the extra thirty miles – the weather was nice and I was in no rush - but I had to recalibrate my route.

Against my better judgment I struck out along the first canal I came across, the Leeds-Liverpool, reasoning that it would be a straightforward way across the Pennines. It led me through or near Blackburn, Accrington and Burnley, all pretty much interchangeable from where I was sitting. I finished for the day up a back lane high above Colne, at a windswept moor-top campsite.

I was just about to put my tent up when the owner asked me if I'd like to stay in the barn. It was a huge, half-timbered construction with massive beams spanning its vast width and seemingly holding the whole thing up. At one end of the building, a couple of comfy-looking sofas flanked a beautiful fireplace. At the other end was a mezzanine which had a full-width curtain concealing real beds. Of course I'd like to stay in the barn. I was the only guest that night, although a friendly black cat wandered in and out at will.

I half-heartedly thought about a wander down the hill to the nearest village's pub, but decided to stay indoors and catch up on some notes. I started reading some of the framed stuff on the wall around the fireplace. A big tableau about the witches from nearby Pendle caught my eye. The illustrations were accompanied by snippets of writing explaining their crimes and trial. Most of it had been written by Potts, a clerk at Lancaster Assizes court, who spoke of:

THE WONDERFULL DISCOVERIE OF WITCHES IN THE COUNTIE OF LANCASTER

Potts goes on to explain their discovery, misdemeanours and capture, taking especial glee in their punishment:

you ſhall all goe from hence to the Caſtle, from whence you came; from thence you ſhall bee carried to the place of Execution for this Countie; where your bodies ſhall bee hanged untill you be dead;
AND GOD HAVE MERCIE VPON YOVR SOVLES

The voice then switched to the most notorious witch of the group, Elizabeth Sowtherns, also known as Demdike, who had died while awaiting trial. Just before her death, she wrote a confession, explaining how to make and use a picture of clay, a tool similar to a voodoo doll:

and when you would have the whole body to conſume away then take the ſayd Picture and burne it and ſo therevpon by that means the body ſhall die

Feeling suddenly alone and chilly in the empty old barn, I slept fitfully on one of the sofas next to the fireplace. There was no way I was going up on that mezzanine to sleep behind a red velvet curtain. I awoke in the early hours to something gently, but insistently, stroking my face. Screaming like a little girl, I jumped clean out of my sleeping bag. The cat jumped higher.

The subsequent early start meant that I was back in York by the middle of the afternoon. That was the sum total of the cycling for September: Barrow and back via Preston. Four home matches in a row meant a sustained period off the bike.

It made for a curious, listless month. Four weeks out of the saddle, unable to take advantage of glorious September weather. My muscles began to atrophy. My once-diminishing beer belly started to make a tentative reappearance. All this time off left me fidgety and unsure. Would I be able to regain all that hard-fought fitness? Would I twang an under-used hamstring? Would September's blue skies turn to grey as soon as I turned a pedal?

Of course I would, I bloody hope not, of course they would.

Kettering Town arrived at Bootham Crescent as the league's second-placed side. They were pretty easily beaten, Brodie twice tapping in flicked-on corners from within the six-yard box. Ferrell's second-half corners had been met by centre backs Parslow and Sangaré. The latter was once again a swaggering presence in defence, sweeping up Kettering's attacks with ease and sauntering into midfield and beyond at will. More performances like this and injured first-choice centre back Dave McGurk would struggle to regain his place.

The match finished 2-0. We were becoming tricky to beat, but pessimism still held sway on the terraces. We were too reliant on Brodie's goals. Foyle's tactics were too negative. A couple of key injuries and the wheels would come off. This is York, after all.

One York fan was starting to get a little nervous about our upturn in fortunes. Sando is one of a group of York City exiles who play five-a-side football on a Monday night in Brixton. He has been watching York since a 1-1 home draw with Aldershot in 1979. In a desperate attempt to divert him from a life of misery, his Mum tried to put him off going to that match by telling him that it was a possible target for the IRA. Well, they had killed Airey Neave the day before. He checked underneath his friend's Grandad's car for bombs at the end of the game, but managed to escape Bootham Crescent with nothing more serious than a lifelong attachment to very average lower-league football. Sando and I had met at the fateful Crawley away match last season and he invited me down to play on a Monday night. I ended up wheezing unconvincingly around the pitch on a weekly basis.

After my last appearance before setting off, we struck a bet. Buoyed by pre-season signings and a couple of pints of Guinness, I confidently predicted that we'd finish in the top eight. We had barely staved off relegation the season before. Sando bit my hand off. If I lost, I had to vote Labour. If Sando lost, he promised to pedal the last away leg of the season with me. The wager was made before the fixture list came out. When it was published, Sando's potential fate was sealed: a trip to Stevenage, 180 miles or so. He hadn't been on a bike for twenty-five years.

Sando's natural pessimism still came to the fore. He was certain that we still had plenty of time to fall apart. He had seen it happen many, many times before. He is a season ticket holder of many years. He remembers queuing round the block at the age of thirteen for a ticket to the FA Cup replay at Anfield and travelling to the match on his own. A much more regular presence at York games than I am, he has only missed a few matches each season since he started supporting them as a kid. When you take all that into account, his natural pessimism starts to look like realism.

Sando was certain we would lose the next home match against a strong Cambridge United side. It was the first proper night match of the season, the sky shining a lovely rich blue under floodlights from the start. After a reasonable opening twenty minutes from York, Cambridge set the tempo and maintained it. Their quick, sharp, incisive midfield swarmed all over us. We were very fortunate to be 1-0 up at half-time, Gash finishing well when the ball broke to him in the box. Later on, he attempted an ambitious overhead kick in front of the Longhurst stand, connecting sweetly with the still night air. It was as close as I came to seeing a successful bicycle kick all season.

The defence was called into constant action after the break, with Sangaré once again very solid. He had to be; Cambridge totally overran us, dominating a comically lopsided second half, sauntering at will through our sadly Lawless-less midfield. We looked to be heading for an unlikely three points when two well-taken goals in three minutes undid us. Jai Reason got the first and took it upon himself to slide triumphantly towards the home fans on his knees, like a returning player settling a score. An absurd celebration. Our supporters got equally absurdly het up about it. Pure pantomime.

A thumping header from Gash rescued a thoroughly undeserved point. It was harsh on Cambridge's excellent supporters, who came in good numbers and sang heartily throughout. Sangaré was undisputed man of the match; his calm defending contributed to us salvaging something from a game we would have lost at any point over the last couple of years.

For the Kidderminster match a few days later, we took our place right on kick-off amongst a decent crowd, considering it was the third home match in ten days. I was still getting my bearings, drinking in the sunshine and scanning the pitch for the returning Lawless, who had been disappointingly confined to the bench, when we conceded. Parslow was similarly distracted, allowing himself to be pick-pocketed on the edge of the box by Duane Courtney. Brian Smikle headed home the resultant cross with relish. We were 1-0 down before the match had really even begun.

In the ninth minute, Brodie burst into the box before being subjected to a protracted and unusually vigorous strip-search by Caines. Despite all this frisking and probing, our ruddy-cheeked hero still somehow managed to get his shot away. The referee played a good advantage before pointing to the spot when Brodie's shot bounced back off the post. Astonished to be red-carded for his last-ditch assault, Caines entered into a debate with the referee which lasted longer than his actual appearance. Unperturbed throughout this lengthy pantomime, Brodie eventually converted low and hard to Coleman's right. The Harriers keeper was sufficiently impressed to shake his hand at the next corner. It had been a frenetic start to the match, and a bad ten minutes to miss. My mate Steve's rueful nod of the head on his arrival confirmed that his last pint in the Bay Horse had caused him to do just that.

Just after the half-hour mark, sustained pressure around the Kidderminster box (or 'fannying around', as the serial moaners around us were sagely musing) led to Sangaré cantering free on the right and wrapping his foot round a sumptuous cross which took Coleman out of the equation. An unmissable chance for Brodie, who showed his contempt for its simplicity, eschewing the easy header and electing instead to caress it home with his left tit. His ninth goal of what was turning into a promising season. The rest of the half was played out without much incident, other than referee Curry rolling back the years to allow Coleman to pick up a quite deliberate back-pass.

Adam Smith started the second half as he had played throughout the first, terrorising the Kidderminster defence with quick, direct running and terrorising passing birds with his astonishingly wayward crossing. On the hour, the stars he'd previously been aiming for aligned and he dinked a lovely cross straight on to Gash's head. Gash scored easily to put us 3-1 up with half an hour to play against ten tiring men. Everything was in place for us to go on and rack up a big score. Less complicated teams would have done just that.

As has become tradition over recent seasons, we attempted to concede as soon as possible after the restart. After a few minutes' spirited reversing and backing off, we succeeded. A free-kick was given away in a central position about twenty-five yards out. Kidderminster's WWII field general Matthew Barnes-Homer sized it up. He struck it very slowly along the ground. Mesmerised by its myriad bobbles and possibly comatose by the time it reached him, Ingham somehow contrived to allow the ball through first his hands then his legs. Even though his flailing limbs took away what little pace the shot possessed, the ball still spluttered inexorably on before apologising over the line.

A nervy half hour ensued. Ingham found himself increasingly involved, with routine through balls causing him constant alarm. He flapped at a couple of crosses in quick succession, redeeming himself moments later with a fantastic trademark one-handed save, to which the York fans are well accustomed.

We were clinging on towards the end, which is testament to how well Kidderminster coped with the arduous task of playing eighty-one minutes with ten men. If it had been eleven-a-side for the whole match, we would have lost our unbeaten home record. As it was, three more stolen points pushed us back into a play-off position. Gash and Brodie had now knocked in thirteen goals in the last six matches. We were up to fifth in the league. Sando would never admit it, but he was getting nervous.

OCTOBER

A month off the bike had left me twitchy and nervous. All this inaction had started to transmit itself to how I felt about the team. I was pretty sure our recent good run would end against Stevenage. They were sitting one place above us in fourth, with a similar record. I was convinced that our unbeaten home record would soon lie in tatters. And all because I'd not done any cycling. Clearly a pathetically solipsistic viewpoint, but I was finding it increasingly difficult to divorce the two elements of the challenge in my mind. I had never been to this many consecutive games.

What must it be like for those who traipse to every match, home and away, season after season after season? Do they believe that their every routine, thought and tic is liable to influence the result? Or do they, like Sando, adopt a more phlegmatic stance? His expectations are now so low that each fresh embarrassment, each new nadir, comes as no surprise. He's seen us beat Arsenal; force extra time at Anfield; get clobbered by Canvey Island; stuffed by St Albans, and every shade of result in between. Supporters like him have made it through all this glory and woe and nonsense to realise that the inner workings of their minds hold no sway whatsoever over the fortunes of a largely rubbish football team. For the sake of my sanity, I had to force myself to think along the same lines.

Stevenage probably would win, because they were a bit better than us. In Steve Morison they had the best striker in the league, who had scored one and made one last time we played. That the last encounter was at Wembley was testament to how Martin Foyle had managed to turn things around since his appointment. Having just about kept us up and got us to the FA Trophy final in the first few months of his tenure, he had kicked on with a solid start to this season. I would be happy if we somehow snaffled a draw to chase away the lingering demons of May's abject Wembley humiliation.

With no miles to make between matches, I had spent a week in Oxford with Jola. Amongst other things, we talked about my trip. She understood why I wanted to do the cycling, but couldn't really get her head round the football side of things. This was disappointing, as I'd really pulled out all the stops to indoctrinate her into being a York fan. I'd taken her to two matches, both in Thames estuary hell-holes, one of which I'd made her cycle to. What more did she want?

A few years back, she had watched Dagenham brush us aside on their way to winning the league. The highlight for Jola was one of their strikers missing from a yard out. Not just the goal, but the ball. Last season, I coaxed her into pedalling from London to Ebbsfleet in the rain. The drizzle turned to hail shortly before kick-off. It fell hard enough that we were moved from the open terrace to the main stand in order to shelter from it. The match was indescribably poor, even by Conference standards. It was a study in boredom, a ninety-minute staring contest. At half-time she asked if the players were paid for doing this.

She'd been at work for this season's opener at Oxford and had managed to wriggle out of other suggested games, but a family Christmas meant that she'd have little chance of getting out of completing her hat-trick of appearances at the home Boxing Day match against Mansfield. That was nearly three months away, but I was already intrigued as to what new depths our boys might plumb.

After the week in Oxford, we said our goodbyes at the station and I boarded the train to York. It carved up the miles; Derby to York in little over an hour. After the Stevenage match I would be setting out on the reverse journey, bound for Tamworth via Derby. It would probably take me a day and a half. Maybe longer, judging by the trees outside the window bent double into the pitiless southerly wind. I hated the wind more than anything. Pedalling through rain was strangely pleasant; cold weather posed no problem either once the first couple of miles had warmed me up. But the wind - the hateful, implacable wind - stung eyes and hands and heart. The train pushed on to York, indifferent to the gale at its back, but I knew we still had battles unresolved.

It's difficult to admire how Graham Westley sends his teams out to play. A team full of big, strong bruisers are drilled in merciless training sessions to bully, harass and time-waste their way to victory. It works for Stevenage, but it would be a lot easier to respect them if they relied more heavily on the talent at their disposal, of which they have plenty. Westley's motto is "attitude is more important than ability". It's a shame because his players have a fair bit of ability married to a dreadful attitude. It's easy to blame the players when you see them carrying out his orders, but they are only playing in his mould.

Westley was manager of Farnborough when they drew Arsenal in the fourth round of the FA Cup. The tie was controversially switched to Highbury at Farnborough's request, meaning an estimated windfall of £500k; a lucrative move for them. Well, for him. Westley quit for Stevenage a few days after the match. As well as being manager, he was also the chairman and majority shareholder at Farnborough. The club didn't see much of the money. He took his backroom staff and most of the team with him. Unsurprisingly, he's not thought of too highly in that particular corner of Hampshire.

Stevenage sacked Westley in May 2006 when they failed to make the play-offs. After a mini-tour of Northamptonshire, taking in jobs at Rushden & Diamonds and

Kettering, he found himself back at the Stevenage helm two years later to "finish the job he'd started". You have to admire his obstinacy, if nothing else.

His team flung themselves at us with typical gusto and a tense, tight affair ensued. Half an hour in, our captain and centre back Danny Parslow rose highest to guide a firm header into the net in front of his adoring fans in the Longhurst. Past Ingham. Stevenage had their lead and they set about defending it in typical snarly fashion.

Scott Laird played as if he were a poster boy for the Westley regime. Before the goal, Stevenage's left back had chopped winger Adam Smith down twice in the opening minutes. His foul count had been rising ever since. After the goal, he divided his time equally between feigning a variety of temporarily career-threatening injuries and clattering into our players with impunity. The lax ref eventually booked him at some point in the second half for his umpteenth scythe.

Our equaliser came in the fifth minute of stoppage time. Laird time. It was a nice irony that the full three points were snatched away from them during the extra minutes that all their time-wasting had accrued. Sangaré rose to head in a Barrett corner to cap another excellent display and cement his nascent cult status. A last-minute equaliser that felt as good as a win. The Longhurst went mental. It's a reflection on the thin gruel served up over recent years, but I hadn't heard celebrations that loud for ages. The players trooped off with "Allez! Allez! Sangaré!" ringing in their ears.

The next day, I set off on the long trek to Salisbury, via a midweek match at Tamworth. Dad joined me again for the first few miles. My legs hurt an awful lot. The month off the bike really had taken its toll. My thigh muscles ached an unreasonable amount and my right hip had developed a worryingly audible click at the apex of each pedal turn. Someone somewhere had a picture of clay of me. Probably Scott Laird.

Thanks to Ernest Marples and Dr Beeching's 1960s rape of the railways, we pootled down the dead straight bike track between York and Selby before Dad turned back and I clicked on to Worksop. Like many smallish towns all over the country, it's a regrettable identikit mishmash of fried chicken outlets, charity shops and bookies. Thrown into the mix is a palpable air of ennui and menace. I've got nothing against Worksop, it's not even that bad, but when a town has had its guts and industry ripped out and replaced by the square root of zero it is likely to feel a little bereft. For Worksop, read Bedford or Hinckley or Wellingborough or any number of similar mid-sized towns which have had their industries looted and their souls pecked away.

Deliberately skirting Mansfield in the morning for reasons outlined above, my stupid bike led me unerringly to Strawberry Bank, Nottinghamshire's highest point. This sort of thing happened with tiresome frequency: what seemed an innocuous shortcut on my contour-free map would inevitably turn out to be an hour-long slog up a ten per cent gradient. When this happened – at least once a day – I would think of Bernard Hinault's attitude to riding. Known as The Badger due to his tenacious attitude, he summed up his philosophy thus: *Tant que je respire, j'attaque.*

I'm not suggesting that there's any link between Hinault, five times champion of the Tour de France, and me, five times champion of the Tour de Pies. That would be an outlandish claim: Hinault would never keep up on the pie front. But there are some similarities, in terms of attitude, if not ability. I'm a dreadful climber, especially with a fully-laden bike, but I'm bloody stubborn. So I continue to attack the hills even when my breathing starts to sound more like a death rattle.

My 'technique' for coping with inclines is to drop it into the granny gear, fix my eyes on a distant marker - *NOT the horizon, please God no, not the horizon, look how far away it is* - and aim for it. When I get to this chosen point I decide on another landmark, a roadside flower or perhaps an oil patch, and aim for that. With grim inevitability, the markers become closer and closer to each other, like the beeps of a metal detector approaching treasure, until by the brow of the hill I'm progressing by individual grains in the tarmac. By these laboured means I conquer dozens of tricky little hills every day. These incremental victories over England's topography are akin to the strangely constipated feeling of watching York try to grind out a result.

An overnight pit-stop at my sister's in Derby left me a few short wind-hampered miles from Tamworth. I'd been to the Lamb Ground just once before, back in 2006. Living in Derby at the time, I went to the match by conventional means. Having run to the ground from the station when the delayed train eventually arrived, I still managed to arrive at the match a sweaty mess. At least this time I had an excuse.

Back then we were riding high and Tamworth, well, weren't. The match ended up a disappointing 2–2 draw, with Clayton Donaldson getting both of our goals. I don't remember much else about the game other than that we went ahead twice and were pegged back almost immediately both times. Even this memory might be wildly inaccurate. The result didn't disrupt our season too much, as we still went on to finish the season in the play-offs, giving ourselves a fresh shot at humiliation.

Morecambe beat us over two legs, drawing 0-0 at the Crescent, then capitalising on some pathetic goalkeeping by Tom Evans to win 2-1 at home. Top-scorer Donaldson was stretchered off in his last game for York before scurrying up to Edinburgh to play for Hibs. A pretty straightforward clause in his contract, that shouldn't have been overlooked, allowed them to sign him for free. Manager Billy McEwan had a shaky start to the following campaign and was replaced by Colin Walker, a Wallace & Gromit extra with all of Nick Park's characters' inane smiles and none of their animation. A close shave with relegation did for him, and in came Foyle. If we don't go up this season he'll be lucky to survive a dodgy run of results next time round. Thus the miserable cycle of non-league existence is perpetuated.

I checked into a B&B on an extravagant whim and strolled into town for a pre-match drink with my sister's husband and some of his mates who'd driven from Derby, and Dave, an old University friend now living in Birmingham. Thanks to Tamworth's Dave

Clayton and Rod Hadley, I had a ticket for the match and an interview and charity cheque presentation on the pitch beforehand. A quick pint turned into three, the last of which swirled around in my belly as I ran to make kick-off. I snuck in through a side entrance, where a Doncaster scout was milling around.

'Not here to see Brodie are you?'

He raised a languid Moorian eyebrow. 'Might be.'

Well if he hadn't heard about him before, he certainly had now. What an idiot. Why didn't I tip him off about Simon Russell, on loan from us to Tamworth, instead? Cursing myself, I sprang through an open door and out onto the pitch, nearly tripping over a man I half-recognised on the way. I had just about enough time before kick-off to stumble out onto the pitch and through a few words before rejoining the rest of my group in the stand.

Some calamitous defending from both sides made for an exhilarating encounter. For most of the first half, Tamworth were much the better side and deservedly led through an excellent Tait header. The right back thought he had doubled his tally and the lead but his thunderous twenty-five-yarder was ruled out for a trip on Sangaré, a fraction before he struck it. For the majority of the first period, we were pulled all over the park by Tamworth's fluid passing, led by the mightily impressive Alex Rodman.

Tamworth's dominance didn't yield the goals that it should have, and they were pegged back when we put together an incongruously fluent move which resulted in Ferrell notching his first of the season with a confident strike low to the keeper's right. For the remaining five minutes of the half, York had the upper hand and were unfortunate not to go in at the break 2 -1 up, Sangaré's header being cleared off the line.

Half-time was improved immeasurably by the discovery of a tiny bar behind the stand so we knocked back a quick pint, garnished with several flies which had parachuted in from the freshly-painted ceiling. We stepped back out onto the terrace just in time to see Smith's surging run release Rankine, who nearly broke the post in two from an acute angle. Just after the hour mark we went ahead, Brodie nodding in unmarked from Ferrell's excellent cross. Hopefully the Doncaster scout was looking away at the time. Ingham attempted to level the scores moments later, charging crazily out to the corner flag in an uncharacteristic lapse. I'm not sure how many more lapses he's allowed this season before they become characteristic. My Dad blames every goal on Ingham, or Ingram as he steadfastly and obtusely insists on calling him. His perceived indiscretions make my Dad blind to his qualities as a 'keeper, namely the high number of excellent saves he makes in each match. It's a good job Dad wasn't there, he'd have been straining at the leash to blame some more dropped points on an Ingham mistake.

Tamworth somehow failed to capitalise on this one. On seventy-eight minutes we went further ahead, the indomitable Sangaré stooping to head home from another Ferrell cross. The mercurial Frenchman now had two in two, and a chance to complete his hat-trick against his former club on Saturday.

To Tamworth's credit they refused to buckle, despite being unluckily behind. With two minutes remaining, Tait grabbed his second of the match with a looping header. Five minutes of added time were produced from nowhere, in which the hosts were very unlucky not to equalise; wayward shooting and several legitimate penalty claims iffily waved away put paid to their unbeaten home record. A fortunate three points catapulted us back up to fourth with a game in hand on most teams. That game in hand was at title favourites Luton, but on recent evidence, we had nothing to fear in this league.

Over a copious breakfast at the Belmont Guest House, I got chatting to Bob Davis of Wessex Archaeology, who was staying in town for a few days to undertake a survey at the castle. He kindly invited me up to have a look round the courtyard, which was closed to the public due to the ongoing works. With plenty of time to play with, I took him up on his offer. As I was leaving their guest house, the owners collared me in the hallway and gave me back most of my money, keeping sufficient to cover the breakfast and insisting that I donate the rest to the cause. This kind gesture was reproduced in some form or other pretty much every day that I was on the road. Offers of a bed for the night; a corner of a garden for my tent; a meal; a pint; a fiver hastily stuffed in my cycling glove: "for your pot, son", "get yourself a pint, mate".

These acts of kindness were nicely summed up by a guy I met a few years previously as I cycled between Land's End and John O'Groats. Again, I was collecting donations for the Alzheimer's Society along the way. I camped for the night at the aptly-named No Man's Land farm, somewhere in Devon's back of beyond. In the morning a man came out of the caravan next to me, gave me a cup of tea and told me he was going to pay for my pitch, saying:

'It's not going to break me and it's not going to make you and it's a sorry tale either way if it does.'

Imagining myself to be a Knight, I pedalled up to the door of Tamworth Castle. It would have been more fitting to fly across a drawbridge, but I had to knock on the door for Bob to let me in. He showed me around the courtyard in which he was conducting his painstaking work.

'It's a motte and bailey castle, like many Norman castles were of course.'

I nodded to mask my ignorance.

'As you can see, there are several different periods of architecture represented.'

The courtyard was indeed surrounded by buildings in a variety of architectural styles.

'That portico over there was added prior to the visit of King James. And over here is where we're doing the survey.'

Bob wandered over to some apparatus that he had set up just inside the castle wall. He showed me the results of his careful sifting, cataloguing and recording: dug-out trenches, half-uncovered foundations, boxes full of filtered soil.

'It looks like something off Time Team.'

'Funny you should say that. We do loads of the pre-work for them. They keep asking me to present for them, but I can't.'

'Why not?'

'I just don't want to do it.'

Like a few of his anecdotes, it started brightly and then just petered out. I was probably keeping him from his work. I mounted my steed, bade him farewell, roared down the ramp and set out to battle with the A51 to Kingsbury.

I made my way to the beautifully-named Meriden, which purports to be the centre of England, and has a medieval sandstone phallus monument to back up its claims. I stopped for a while at the nearby National Cyclists' Memorial, built to commemorate those cyclists who died during the First and Second World Wars. The memorial was erected with subscriptions from cyclists and cycling clubs following a public meeting held in October 1919. They decided to plonk it in Meriden to make it more accessible for cyclists to reach, no matter where they were in the country.

Maybe the monument accounted for the fair number of cyclists zipping along the surrounding backroads. I rode a while with John, who kindly halved his pace so that I could keep up with him. John competes in the West Midlands Cyclo-Cross League and was out on his winter bike for a recovery ride. A few days before, he had been flying across rutted fields and through rivers, carrying his mud-spattered bike when the going got too tough to pedal. His recovery ride consisted of a fifty-mile loop at twice the pace I could possibly muster. I was half his age. He turned for home somewhere near Royal Leamington Spa and I plodded on to Banbury. I rolled into Oxford just as darkness fell.

I'm sure there's a stunning view from the top of the Ridgeway, the footpath that straddles the chalk ridge which runs from Wiltshire to Ivinghoe Beacon in Buckinghamshire. After the gap at Goring, the same ridge runs most of the way to The Wash. I would struggle over it many more times in the coming months. This part of the path cuts diagonally across Southern England, and has been in continuous use by tradesmen, armies, drovers, and now walkers and cyclists for the last 5,000 years. I climbed the ridge to the west of Wantage and rode along its spine for a few muddy miles before dropping down the other side and coasting down to Lambourn through lovely rolling countryside adorned with white-railed training gallops.

The weather was grim. A southerly wind lashed my face with icy rain. I had another forumer to meet in Salisbury. Forumer moist (the lower-case being intentional) had offered to meet me for a couple of pints and show me round town when I got there. I would be as wet as his name by the time I arrived. The football forum isn't solely confined to football; indeed threads spring up on all manner of subjects. For a year or so, a few aspiring writers had been posting stories for each other to read and critique. As much as is possible between faceless internet geeks, a decent rapport had built up.

moist was one of the writers, a Liverpool fan from Reading who lives in a village near Salisbury. An original glory hunter, he grew up in an era of Liverpool sweeping all before them, and has supported them ever since. Plenty of my friends did the same; boyhood Everton and Liverpool fans brought up on the unbroken success of their 1980s heydays. It's difficult to get too worked up about them supporting a team to which they have no geographical connection – they have all stuck with the Merseyside giants, long after the glory has faded: the season after York had knocked Manchester United out of the League Cup, we disposed of Everton at the same stage for no reason other than we were simply the better side.

moist called me just after I'd done an interview for BBC Wiltshire, sheltering under a tree on the village green in Durrington? Netheravon? One of them. The one with the great big tree on the green.

'How are you getting on?'

'I'm soaked. Probably about an hour away.'

'Do you know where you're staying?'

'There's a municipal campsite just outside town. I'll stick my tent up and head into town to meet you.'

'I wouldn't be camping in this if I were you. A friend of mine runs a really nice B&B just north of town.'

'I can't afford to do that, mate.'

'You don't have to.'

He wouldn't let me pay for most of the Guinness we drank in The Cloisters either.

'Think of it as my sponsorship, I think it's pretty amazing what you're doing. I thought you'd appreciate a comfy bed for the night. Hopefully someone somewhere will do something similar for me or mine at some point.'

I thanked him. 'I really appreciate it. I wasn't looking forward to the tent tonight at all. So, did you not feel a bit apprehensive about meeting a complete stranger from the internet?'

'It felt weird at first but the more I thought about it, the more I felt comfortable with it. There seems to be a happy camaraderie in the writing thread. I've read enough of your stuff to suggest I needn't be worried about meeting some strange internet weirdo with no social skills.'

moist's stories are very well-written, claustrophobic tales of vampires and the unheimlich, but that hadn't put me off meeting him either. As we queued for a taxi at the end of the night, his neighbour pulled us into the adjacent Spirit Bar. He seemed to know most people in the place, hence the town's nickname of Smallsbury. The Spirit Bar had a multi-coloured patchwork dancefloor which lit up in time to the music like an enormous Simon toy. I couldn't take my eyes off it. Or my feet for that matter: it was covered in a gloopy film of spilled drink. Mostly my sambuccas.

I'd never been to Salisbury before, so I cleared my head in the morning by wandering around the cathedral. Well, round the cloisters anyway. I had nowhere to leave the burden of a bike so propped it up against the ancient limestone wall and wandered round the incredible vaulted quad. Looking up at the tree in the middle of the lawn and the cathedral's great soaring central spire beyond, I felt the last traces of an aniseed hangover float away.

I met my cousin Adam, son of my real Uncle Graham, before the match and we made our way to the ground together.

'Have you been to see Bid yet?'

Bid, or Biddy, is our Gran, and she'd recently spent a few days in hospital while they carried out some checks. Although outwardly robust for her eighty-nine years, the trips to the District had been getting more frequent.

'Not yet mate, no. I'll go see her before the Oxford match.'

'She might be back home by then, she looked as strong as ever when I saw her.'

'Let's hope so, it'll be nice to see her noseying on the neighbours from her chair again.'

The Oxford home revenge job was on the following Saturday, but first we had to dispose of Salisbury, which on recent form seemed feasible. At the ground, the Salisbury general manager and Southampton legend Nick Holmes let us in and showed me where to store my bike. An FA Cup winner with the Saints, he was still in good shape and retained an aura of success. When I'd called the club beforehand, it was Nick who answered, and he was as personable in real life as he had been on the telephone.

He had to run off on one of many pre-match errands. 'I'll buy you a drink in the bar afterwards. Let's hope it's a good match.'

It wasn't. Sangaré undid some of his recent good work by hacking their striker Tubbs down for a penalty in the first couple of minutes. The prolific Tubbs picked himself up and converted it. Bittner in the Salisbury goal comfortably dealt with everything we threw at him thereafter, and finished as an obvious man of the match. Our ten-match unbeaten run gone just like that. I'd cycled 300 miles in the wind and rain to see my team lose in a corrugated shed on the edge of a soulless industrial estate. All that remained was to turn round and pedal back.

Adam and I found ourselves in the bar, where Nick was as good as his word, buying a couple of pints for us both. Despite being in great demand, he made time to chat away with us. As did a familiar-looking dark-haired bloke by his side, who turned out to be the Salisbury manager, former Southampton player Tommy Widdrington. It was only as I was pitching my tent, having decided to stay the night at the municipal campsite, that I realised he was the guy I'd tripped over earlier on that week in my haste to get on the Tamworth pitch.

As I crested the Ridgeway on the way back to Oxford, I passed another solo cyclist coming the other way. We both gave an almost imperceptible nod, lacking the puff to do anything other than silently acknowledge the other's achievement. Hitting forty mph on the way back down, I freewheeled what seemed like most of the way to Oxford.

With my lights failing I barrelled down the tree-lined riverside bike path, clattering over unseen exposed roots, scaring myself witless with every snapped twig. I was meeting Jola in Isis, an atmospheric Thameside pub a short wander, ride or row from Oxford city centre. Propping the bike against the pub wall, I went to turn off the rear light and noticed that from the back, the bike and its bags were all jowly and slouchy. A victim of dislocation back in August; now it had suffered a stroke. Those snapping sounds hadn't all been twigs: the fork had gone again.

You should never go back. But like Steve Coppell and Crystal Palace, I just couldn't resist. I just couldn't leave the Kona Sutra alone. You'd think I would have learnt from our first separation. The Ridgeback had given a great account of itself since its introduction as a replacement to cover the Kona's early injury. It's a lovely machine, solid and dependable; understated silver to the Kona's look-at-me bright green. It got the job done with the minimum of fuss, without resorting to flashiness. The Ray Wilkins of tourers, to the Sutra's Glenn Hoddle.

With wearying predictability, I had turned my back on the Ridgeback as soon as I took delivery of the replacement Sutra frame. Kitted out with a sturdier rack and honeyed Brooks bar tape to match the saddle, it was a green goddess once more, positively winking at me from the corner of the room in anticipation of our future adventures. Well, we'd managed the sum total of a trip to Barrow and back and just over half of a trip to Salisbury and back before the new frame snapped in exactly the same position as its predecessor. It's clearly a design fault; a steel frame tourer shouldn't give way just like that. I could almost hear the trusty Ridgeback sniggering away in York in its cupboard under the stairs.

I could hardly rely on Ridgeback digging me out of a hole this time round. I had to get from Oxford to York in two days for the biggest game of the season so far, coincidentally against league leaders Oxford.

Kona could send the frame off to a specialist welding firm to cobble together some Heath Robinson solution, but it would take weeks. There were no more replacement frames; I had the last one in the country. It was unrideable with the rear rack on, so I decided to leave my panniers at Jola's and ride back to York with the essentials in a backpack. And hope that the crack didn't spread.

How I hated the flighty, unpredictable, beautiful beast. How quickly our love had turned sour. I kept glancing over at it, sulking in the corner of Jola's back yard, locked up next to her flatmate's tiny pink Raleigh Prima. I had as much chance of riding that from Oxford to York - a fanciful child's bike with a broken crank.

If I somehow managed to make it back intact, I would dust down solid, dependable Ridgeback Wilkins again. Kona Hoddle will be confined to the cupboard under the stairs, atoning for sins committed in its previous life.

No panniers meant no tent. I had to rely on getting a bed for a couple of nights. A fruitless attempted re-weld and general dilly-dallying led to a late start so I decided to call in another forum favour. I set off to meet Bob Rhinestone.

Forumer Rhinestone is from a small village near Banbury. I only knew two things about him: he was a QPR fan and he was cycling round the world. He was two years into his quest – about halfway through. Many kind people had been putting him up for the night all over the globe, and his family wanted to return the favour, which is how I ended up in the village pub waiting for his Dad, Bob, to meet me.

It quickly became apparent that Rhinestone had inherited his love of QPR from his Dad. Over a pint, Bob told me how he grew up in Primula Street on the White City Estate, less than a mile from Loftus Road. After a brief, unseemly flirtation with Chelsea, which we can discount on the grounds of youth, he was dragged along by his two uncles to see his local team. It was an instant, permanent conversion. He still went to Chelsea, specifically to boo Peter Osgood. Not many kids these days could afford to indulge such a magnificently singular obsession. But every other Saturday he stood with his two uncles at Loftus Road, until he bought a wooden rattle and they insisted on familial segregation.

His timing was impeccable. Soon after Bob started going to Loftus Road, Jim Gregory took over as chairman and set about turning the club's fortunes around. Rodney Marsh's arrival from Fulham helped them to the Third Division championship and, incredibly, the League Cup in the same 1966-1967 season. The maverick Marsh scored forty-four goals in fifty-three games. When stuff like that happens in your first full season as a supporter, you're bound to form a lasting bond with the club.

After dinner at the Rhinestone ranch, Bob started to show me his impressive collection of QPR programmes. They were naturally arranged in alternating blue and white plastic folders, in season order. Most of the seasons' folders were complete. The folders took up two full shelves of a bookcase. It's a serious collection. We spent a fruitless half hour trying to find a mid-1980s programme from a QPR v York League Cup tie, but couldn't pin down the year. We settled on 1984, but still couldn't find it. Bob did his best to hide his disappointment at its omission.

To give him some time to get over it, I tried to move the subject away from football.

'How did Matt first broach the subject of heading off around the world?' Well, I could hardly call him Rhinestone to his Dad.

'The simple answer is that he didn't tell us. He told us he was going to cycle to Vietnam for Christmas. Both Carol and I wondered if he had something else in mind but we never envisaged anything approaching the scale of what he's doing.'

Matt had set off from home two years before, heading across Europe and on through Kazakhstan and China. He then looped round South East Asia, back up the Chinese coast and into Japan, where he boarded a boat for Alaska. He was currently battling huge, menacing roadtrains for room on the highway. He still had the whole of the west coast of Canada and the USA to negotiate, before dropping into Mexico and Central and

South America. The plan was to get another boat from Terra del Fuego to South Africa, then pedal all the way up to Egypt, skip across the Middle East and back home through Europe. And what had I achieved? I'd pottered around on some B roads and snapped two frames in the process. Pathetic.

'We're worried about him at times, of course. But he's learnt so much along the way. He was clueless about fixing stuff before he went, but he's become really self-sufficient. There have been times when we've not received an expected call from him, which is concerning, but I also believe there are a lot of really good people out there who will look after my boy when he needs them.'

Bob's concern was understandable, but it was far outweighed by the pride he felt in what his son was doing. It will be an incredible achievement when he makes it back, and his parents will deserve a share of the plaudits for their support.

Bob set me on the road with strong coffee, a big breakfast and best wishes. I hoped to ride with them both one day when Matt returned.

Melton Mowbray and Epworth. Pork pies and John Wesley. A filthy room above a seedy pub and a basic B&B in a one-horse town. The glamour of life on the road.

I paused for a breather in the Cross Keys' car park at the top of Stillingfleet Hill. It's a Samuel Smith's pub which for a long period used to sell their excellent, idiosyncratic beer at £1.08 a pint. The price has since crept up to a scandalous £1.22. The hill is a short, abrupt one which offers the best vantage point in the village. Stillingfleet is centred on a large expanse of common land – The Green - which flanks Stillingfleet Beck, a tributary of the nearby River Ouse. Most of the village's houses face each other across The Green, like pawns on a chessboard. Others line the main road through the village which bisects the village; from above, the dwellings' layout resembles a cross of Saint George.

The Green was our year-round playground. In early spring we would attack the unruly grass with borrowed lawnmowers, taming a rectangle to serve as our football pitch. One year we made rudimentary goal frames with spare wood, painted them white and sank them into hastily-dug holes. They were flimsy affairs which would keel over when struck by even the feeblest of shots.

As spring turned to summer we would set about the middle of the pitch with garden rollers, transforming it into an uneven, and in retrospect, incredibly poor cricket square. To us it was Headingley and we would play there for hours, frequently losing the ball in the untamed grasses and reeds which surrounded the pitch. The unreadable bounce which we blamed for our wayward football shots also helped us to kid ourselves that we could become the next Shane Warne.

We would play both sports all year round unless the floods intervened. Rain from the Yorkshire Dales feeds into the River Ouse which runs through the middle of York. When the city is imperilled by its rising waters, the flood defence system downstream is opened, which in turn inundates Stillingfleet. The tiny beck, usually a benign trickle in which we would fish for dace, roach and chub, swells up to become a lake that covers the whole green.

Undeterred, we would simply use the water as a new toy; paddling in the shallows, learning to skim stones and, as we grew older, setting out on it in canoes. One particularly severe flood led to my Dad and my Uncle Gordon delivering papers and milk in this way, rowing up to the stranded villagers' front doors in their bright green canoe.

Gordon is a virtually-blind basket weaver who still lives on the outskirts of the village. My sister Sally and I would spend hours at his house. He used to hide an elephant figurine somewhere in his labyrinthine garden with money underneath it for us to find. Whoever uncovered it first would sprint off to the village shop and come triumphantly back, pockets bulging with penny sweets.

This shop had been the destination for my first solo cycling adventure. At the age of two, I set off for it on the same four-wheeled bike with which I'd hugged the Heysel touchline when watching my Dad play rugby for Belgium. It was an understated machine – bright yellow wheels and a royal blue body, fronted with a rabbit's face with its ears for handlebars. I was a stylish shopper as a toddler. My frantic Mum was hardly placated when I returned an hour later trilling 'I've been to the shop Mummy, and do you know what? It was closed.'

The floods would often linger through the winter and freeze over. What a brilliant, ever-changing playground we had. Skidding competitions on the ice, back brake locked for what seemed like miles, until the wheels would whip sideways and send us crashing down. Once we took it upon ourselves to have a game of ice football. When it came to my turn in goal I flung myself sideways with customary recklessness to keep out a shot. I landed with a resounding crack. The ice held firm. My head didn't. My friend Matt, an exotic in the village as his family had moved here from Harpenden, took me and my gushing head to see my Mum. She knew as soon as she heard the knock at the front door that something was up; we always used the back door.

Within minutes, our very local GP Dr Smithson was round to patch me up, one of several times he had to perform wonders at short notice. He was also called on when I electrocuted myself on my Dad's dodgy wiring, and packed me off to hospital just before my appendix burst. I very much doubt I'd have made it through my teenage years without him living next-door-but-one.

Our makeshift pitch was bordered by a solitary plane tree, in which we made a treehouse with a rope swing, and a hay cushion underneath to land in. To the right of the pitch was Pam's lovely stone bungalow and huge garden, a magical realm where we ran amok with her consent, playing kiss-catch and hide-and-seek. It stood on the corner of the Back Lane, up which we would disappear every autumn to collect conkers from the woods. We would come back laden down not only with horse chestnuts, but also armfuls of fallen branches to help build the bonfire on the village green. The whole village would join in on the fifth of November. The mums would cook baked potatoes, parkin and soup, then stand back in wry amusement as their husbands wrestled with Catherine wheels, set off horizontal rockets and tried to coax the recalcitrant bonfire back to life.

I lived in Stillingfleet from when I was born until my parents split up just before I went away to University. Every road, hill and field in the vicinity felt subtly different from those I was pedalling through every day. Even the air around me felt unlike it did elsewhere, distorted by fragments of memory and snatches of half-forgotten conversations. I know nowhere else as intimately as here.

I drank in the view from the top of the smallish hill which had seemed so fearsome as a kid. Our much-loved pitch was overgrown, its goals long since dismantled. The village shop had closed down: it's just another house now. No rope swing dangled from the plane tree. Pam's bungalow is no longer there. In its place have sprung up five 'farmhouse-style family homes' which take up every inch of her beautiful garden. The new houses have no gardens. Their prospective buyers are being sold a rural idyll which their very purchase is helping to destroy.

I stopped for a while at the bottom of our old drive, leaning on the gatepost that Grandad would often scrape with his navy Mini Metro on his way in and out. He was gently mocked for his poor driving at the time, but I can't help thinking it was an early, unspotted sign of his Alzheimer's.

There was nothing else to detain me, so I made for Gordon's. He wasn't in. Laden down with the cumbersome rucksack and half a lifetime's memories, I set off for York.

The league leaders lay in wait. Oxford had kicked on from their jammy opening day win and had just moved nine points clear at the top with a 5-0 thrashing of Gateshead.

I nipped in to see Gran before the match. The hospital is just a short stroll from the ground. She seemed in pretty good spirits, full of her usual devil and mischief, and was looking forward to getting home. I told her I'd see her there when I got back up after the Luton match.

Back outside, I made my way along the brick-walled alley and over the railway bridge, becoming along the way a part of a good, loud crowd of well over 4,000, which was treated to that rarest of things at this level: a proper football match. The defences were on top for most of the game, holding firm in the face of all that was thrown at them. Midway through the second half, York took the lead. A good flowing move culminated in the tireless Rankine tapping in Ferrell's excellent cross. A tense twenty minutes followed. Oxford grabbed an equaliser with nine minutes to go, Simon Clist turning in a similar effort to Rankine's. Our left back James Meredith was sent off soon after for a second bookable offence. The Longhurst became fearful, but the opening day robbery wasn't to be repeated. We held on for a deserved point in an excellent game.

We had nothing to fear in this division. We had held our own against the best side in the league. I'm sure I wasn't alone in starting to dream of the play-offs, at the very least.

I set off very late on the Sunday, leaving myself only two-and-a-half days to get to Luton. Once again I took the cycle-path to Selby and then flitted across the back roads to Thorne and beyond, stopping again for the night in Epworth, the birthplace of John Wesley and Methodism.

I found a great road in the morning that followed the course of the Trent to Gainsborough. I picked my way south, skirting round Lincoln and trying to delay the moment when I'd have to go up the ridge onto the top of the Lincolnshire Wolds which lay dark and brooding to the east. I was starting to tire, so aimed for Stamford with the intention of finding a campsite when I got there. The tiny undulating back road I was cycling along took it out of me more than I thought it would. Well short of Stamford, I stopped in the village of Irnham and wandered into the pub. I didn't leave until the morning.

As soon as I walked in, it was clear that the Griffin Inn was a proper village pub. A few locals were engaged in animated conversation at the bar. The glow from a roaring fire mirrored the soft electric light bouncing back off the stone walls. To the right of the chimney, the pub team and their local rivals congregated round the darts board.

A large, jovial man rushed in and out of the kitchen behind the bar with plates of inviting hot food. The lady behind the bar nodded that they had a room, poured me a pint, took my food order and told me to stick the steed out the back. I unsaddled and tethered it and came back in. I got chatting to the locals at the bar; I'd never felt more at home on the road on the whole trip.

The large, jovial man turned out to be Chris, the chef and landlord, and the lady behind the bar was his wife Liz. We chatted together with their eclectic mix of regulars, many of whom had followed Chris and Liz from their previous pub in Ryhall, a dozen miles away. One of these old regulars was Courtney, an American bookshop manager with an unusually good knowledge of cricket who offered for me to stay with her and her husband the next time I was passing through.

A brilliant meal and a couple more pints later, I was ready for what felt like the best rest of the trip so far. I ran myself an incredibly hot bath to try to soothe my right leg, which was still clicking with each pedal turn. Then I sank into the huge bed and didn't move until it was time for an equally huge breakfast. I'd be stopping here again.

A day on the Cambridgeshire and Bedfordshire back roads got me to Luton just in time to meet Will before the match. I stashed the bike in his car as we were heading back to London that night. I'd get the train back to Luton before cycling back to York for the FA Cup fourth qualifying round match with part-timers Bedworth United of the Zamaretto League First Division Midlands. Nothing illustrates the fall into non-league more starkly than having to qualify for the right to take part in the first round proper of the FA Cup.

A good crowd streamed towards Kenilworth Road through the floodlit backstreets. Considering it has hosted top-flight football as recently as 1992, it's an odd little ground. You enter the away end through a gap between two terraced houses, a bit like walking into someone's back yard. A low-slung row of glass-fronted executive boxes runs the length of one touchline, giving the place the feel of the greenhouse section of a large independent provincial garden centre.

A tight first half full of crisp passing and sturdy defending ended with York a goal up, thanks to a well-taken Neil Barrett toe-poke. Luton dominated the second half, Asa Hall hammering home a deserved equaliser half-way through. York clung on for the rest of the match, and nearly snatched an unlikely winner, but substitute Adam Boyes' sole was just a fraction too thin to connect with Brodie's last minute cross.

'You know you don't have to go, don't you?' A disembodied voice drifted in from the next room.

'I do. I said I would.'

'But it's only the qualifying round. It's not important. Nobody will be there, nobody will know.'

'I'll know. I said I'd do all the FA Cup matches. I thought we'd only have one as usual. It was a token gesture. How was I to know we'd draw these cloggers?'

'You tart.' Will's body had made it through to the lounge to join his voice. Tart is one of his favourite words, along with codpiece, ringpiece, scruttocks – a Willism which I think means a kind of hybrid buttocks and scrotum – twat and cock. He uses them freely and somewhat indiscriminately, as much punctuation as insult. Will had given up a week's holiday in April to ride with me from York to Eastbourne. I got the feeling I'd be on the receiving end of the full repertoire.

Will had once again kindly given up his Ealing lounge to me for the night, and his bathroom for the bike. Away from York, I would stay here more often than anywhere else over the next few months. Will is the kindest, fartiest host.

'If you forgot about this nothing match, you'd only need to get the train back to Luton, then pedal down to Crawley. So much easier than cycling Luton to York to Crawley.' Will exited stage right, pursued by a fart.

I took my bike out of his bathroom and stumbled with it down the narrow stairs. Will's voice floated down after me.

'It's only the qualifying round.'

'See you next week. Thanks again, mate.'

I was back in York a couple of days later, having taken Courtney up on her offer on the way back up.

There was no romance to this Cup match. Bedworth were the worst kind of nothing team, with pissed-up fans looking to make a name for themselves by taking on what their tiny minds perceived to be the 'big boys'. Their heroes set out for a nil-nil from the first whistle. They managed this for seven minutes, before Rankine sliced through to score an excellent solo goal. Bedworth then won and missed a penalty;

Brodie scored a second for York just before half time. It stayed that way to the end. A sobering trip back to the Midlands for the Bedworth fans, especially the one dressed only in a Borat mankini.

'Hello, son.'

Gran's familiar smile lit up her face. She hadn't made it back home yet.

'When are we getting you out of here?'

'Oh, soon I hope. I've had enough. I'm fed up.'

'I'm not surprised, it can't be any fun being cooped up in here.'

'It's not.'

Her face lit up again, she never dwells on things, always looks for the positive.

'I think it's canny what you're doing.' Her signature word, canny. It meant all sorts of things, all of them good. 'I got a brochure from the Alzheimer's people the other day. And you were in it. So I rang them up and do you know what I said? I said "that's my Grandson doing all that cycling for you. I'm ever so proud of him." And I am.'

I looked away so she wouldn't see the tears in my eyes. She followed up with a non sequitur.

'I do worry about Jola.'

'She's fine Gran, what are you worried about?'

'I'm worried about her, we all are.' She suddenly looked incredibly tired, and very, very old. She was never usually susceptible to this kind of jumbled talk.

'Get some rest, Gran. The sooner we get you home the better.' We both agreed we'd take care; I kissed her on the forehead and pedalled reluctantly south.

It is 270 miles from York to Crawley. I would rack up 1,200 miles in October alone. Quite often, they would tick by with hardly any incident, as I retraced my wheel-marks from previous trips. This was just such one of those journeys. Before I knew it, I found myself on Halloween in creepy Crawley, back where it all began.

Sometimes in this division, we play in proper old league grounds in front of decent, partisan crowds in interesting towns. And sometimes, fewer than a thousand people turn up to watch in a concrete and steel flat-pack stadium in a concrete and steel flat-pack town. Crawley is awful. Unremittingly grim. If by strange quirk of inertia and circumstance I found myself living there, I'd go to the football to escape the drudgery. Why then do so few of the townsfolk choose to do so? About 700 of them turned up to watch their pretty good team play another half-decent outfit. What's it like in a dead rubber at the end of the season when Histon come to town?

Brodie lit up a dull first half with a fizzing free-kick, in off the post, to give us a half-time lead. Then it all fell apart. Steve Evans' men scored three simple, deserved and unanswered goals to take all three points. Like Evans' fall from grace due to tax evasion when manager of Boston United, it was all a bit brutal and swift. Immediately after the match, the sizeable City South contingent – Will, Sando, Marcus, the Daves and all, made for London by train or car. In a much slower fashion, I set off for the same destination. With the Surrey Hills looming in front of me, I pedalled off into the lonely night.

NOVEMBER

The hundred miles between Bedford and Edwinstowe left little impression on my memory. I know I left Bedford late, skirted Kettering and then zig-zagged off into the Leicestershire hills on some lovely undulating B roads. Somewhere along the way, I ripped a soggy hole in my map and would from now on have to navigate between Newark and Retford by memory and guesswork. I suppose I could replace the map, but I've grown a bit fond of the creased, grubby squares that I've been lifting out of an RAC road atlas and folding into my handlebar bag's transparent pouch. As well as the roads along which I travel, they map out the punctures, the falls and the rhythms of the trip.

The rip was of no consequence for now, as I was lumbering along hilly back roads somewhere west of the hole. I stopped for a steak in a remote village pub north of Melton Mowbray. At some point, I came close to Nottingham's north-eastern suburbs. The rest of the trip was a cold, dark blur until, just before midnight, I saw the lights of Center Parcs twinkling mysteriously in the woods to the left of the A614. It had been a long old day. I felt like Frodo arriving in Lothlórien.

Jola, my Dad and his partner, my sister and her family had booked a break here and the fixture list had thrown up the dumb luck to allow me to spend most of the week with them. I arrived on the Monday evening, staying until the Friday before needing to make a dash for York and the FA Cup first round proper. A few days' lounging around the swimming pool in good company set me up nicely for the Cup tie. It felt like a wise, forgiving manager had given me a few days off training before the big match.

The Kona and I gobbled up the sixty-three miles to York in less than five hours, easily our best performance of the season. I'd been focusing on the coming game since the final whistle at Crawley. A tie against Crewe Alexandra in the FA Cup first round proper felt like a real match. It was only the third such feeling of the season, after Luton away and Oxford at home. This is one of the side-effects of six years of non-league obscurity. This kind of proper match serves as a stark reminder of how much everyday excitement had been lost along with our League status.

Crewe played some good, neat football throughout, and deserved their lead going into the break. The tricky Grant tormented Purkiss and McGurk all afternoon, scoring Crewe's first and making their second for Calvin Zola. In between these goals, Brodie headed in an Adam Smith cross to briefly grant York parity. After soaking up a bit of early second-half pressure as Crewe went in search of a killer third goal, York seemed to collectively move up a gear. They put Crewe under sustained pressure for the last half hour of the match. The Railwaymen defended their lead in the haphazard manner York fans have become accustomed to suffering; eventually they hit the buffers.

After striking a series of comically inept corners, Barrett finally managed to lift one off the floor. The ironic cheers for his mild achievement were still ringing out as Pacquette took it down and fired home, the ball deflecting in off a Crewe defender's outstretched leg on the line for the equaliser. I'd hardly had time to consider the midweek there-and-back over the Pennines that a replay would entail, before Brodie took matters into his own hands and rendered such thinking obsolete, capping off our comeback and his barnstorming run with a fierce, unstoppable strike.

Maybe it was the adrenalin kicking in, but the way he drifted and drifted to the right, beating his man for pace before lashing it home, was slightly reminiscent of Owen's goal against Argentina. Or maybe I had cracked my head a little too hard against someone's flailing elbow celebrating Pacquette's equaliser.

Three minutes later, the ref blew for full time. Memories of every moronic driver who had given me three inches' grace; of each uphill slog into wind and rain; of both snapped frames, all dissolved away the instant the final whistle went. It had been a raucous, exhilarating end to an excellent match in which the visitors had fully played their part.

We drew Cambridge away in the second round. A tricky and disappointing draw, but on recent form a navigable one. Cambridge hadn't really kicked on from their excellent display at Bootham Crescent, and York had been grinding out result after dull, painstaking result. A decent performance at the Abbey Stadium and we'd be just one lucky swirl of the balls away from a stab at repeating our mid-1980s FA Cup exploits.

In those heady days, York reached the FA Cup fifth round twice in consecutive seasons. In 1984-1985 the newly-promoted side beat Blue Star, Hartlepool United and Walsall without conceding a goal, before being drawn against Arsenal at Bootham Crescent in the fourth round. City supporters joined the ground staff in clearing heavy snow off the pitch on the morning of the match. It was piled up high all round the touchlines; in the TV coverage you can see a ballboy crouching on the touchline, flanked by white peaks. Amazingly, City kept their illustrious opponents at bay for the whole match. In fact, they were probably the better side on a skittery, icy pitch. The teams were heading for a replay at Highbury when Keith Houchen, who would later score a flying header to win the FA Cup final for Coventry, intervened. In Jonathan Strange's biography of Houchen, *A Tenner and a Box of Kippers*, the man himself explains the game's decisive moment:

I had made a run and got on the goal-side of Williams when I felt him tugging at my shirt and his arms went round my neck. The referee was only ten yards away when I looked up after going down under the challenge.

I knew it was close to time but didn't know exactly how long there was to go. It seemed to be ages between being fouled and when I was able to take the kick.

The goalkeeper made up my mind for me. I saw him leaning to his left, and so I thought I would have a go at the other corner.

Which he did with some aplomb, striking the ball a foot inside Lukic's post and sending the City fans behind the goal into raptures. Having seen off the might of Arsenal – who had fielded the likes of Lukic, Sansom, Talbot, O' Leary, Mariner, Woodcock and Nicholas - Houchen missed out on a chance to take on an even bigger challenge in the fifth round.

York were drawn at home against Liverpool, at the time arguably the best side in Europe. Houchen was injured for this match, but his teammates held out for a heroic 1-1 draw at Bootham Crescent, with Ricky Sbragia grabbing the equaliser for York. The replay at Anfield brought an abrupt end to City's progression, as the Merseyside giants turned on the style in a crushing 7-0 victory.

Amazingly, the teams met again at the same stage a year later. York had negotiated a unique path to the fifth round, beating four non-league sides along the way. Liverpool once again made the trip across the Pennines to York to contest a place in the quarter-finals. City dominated the first half but failed to make their possession and chances count, and Liverpool were relieved to make it to half-time at 0-0. Just after the hour, Walwyn set up Gary Ford, who slipped it past Grobbelaar to give York the lead. They only held it for a few minutes before Jan Molby converted a penalty given for handball. Once more, the match ended 1-1. There was to be no repeat of the Anfield humiliation in the replay. Indeed, a Canham equaliser took the game to extra time, in which Liverpool struck twice to end York's run once again.

They were an incredible couple of seasons for City fans and team alike. But as remarkable as Denis Smith's team's FA Cup exploits were, they could never match those of the side that turned out in York's colours thirty years before them. In comparison, the 1954-1955 FA Cup run reads like a far-fetched script from a Boy's Own annual.

Back then, non-league sides Scarborough and Dorchester Town were dispatched in the first two rounds, with Arthur Bottom picking up half of the eight goals, his strike partner Norman Wilkinson bagging two of the others. This set up a third round tie at Bloomfield Road against a Blackpool side that had won the FA Cup two years before, beating Bolton Wanderers in the legendary Matthews final. Matthews and Mortensen were amongst eight of that Cup Final side who turned out for the Tangerines against York, who they were widely expected to brush aside.

An even first half was drawing to a close when Syd Storey whipped in a cross which Blackpool goalkeeper Farm misjudged, the ball sailing over his head into the net. Matthews was kept uncharacteristically subdued throughout, and York carried on in the second half as they had in the first. With twenty minutes left, Billy Fenton raced on to a Wilkinson through-ball to double the lead and end the scoring. Third Division

York had won away at top-flight Blackpool, one of the favourites for the Cup. An astonishing result which was at least on a par with the win over Arsenal thirty years later, if not a greater upset. The reward was a tricky tie away at non-league Cup specialists Bishop Auckland. But York were not to slip up, notching a relatively straightforward 3-1 win courtesy of another strike by Storey and two more from Bottom.

The fifth round draw threw up a home match against a mighty Tottenham Hotspur side that included Alf Ramsey and Danny Blanchflower. A packed Bootham Crescent saw Spurs duly take the lead through George Robb after only a few minutes. The run seemed to be coming to a predictable end, but on the half-hour mark the match was turned on its head. A goal each for Wilkinson and Fenton within a minute of each other gave York an unimaginable lead, which they held on to until half-time. Tottenham cranked up the pressure in the second half, but City held firm. With ten minutes left, Wilkinson struck again, knocking a Fenton cross past Reynolds to complete a remarkable 3-1 victory. The crowd streamed on to the Bootham Crescent pitch to mob their heroes, who had emulated the 1938 York side in reaching an FA Cup quarter-final as a third tier side.

An awkward trip to Meadow Lane for the quarter-final against Second Division Notts County awaited. Thousands of York fans made the short journey down to the Midlands in a bullish mood. Their heroes didn't disappoint. A solitary strike from Arthur Bottom was enough to send Third Division York into the semi-finals of the FA Cup.

Dave Batters sums up the return to York in his brilliant reference book *York City: The Complete Record*.

The scenes in the city of York that night were quite incredible. The first of fourteen special trains arrived back at 8.10pm and many people assembled at the station to greet those who had been there. To the roar of rattles, bells and wild cheering, the supporters arrived back in triumph. Red and white favours, top hats, umbrellas, even suits in red and white were everywhere and the station remained a cauldron of noise and excitement until midnight, when the last train arrived.

A fortnight later, 21,000 York fans – a fifth of the city's population – travelled to Hillsborough to see City take on Newcastle United in the semi-final. The First Division Magpies fielded the likes of Jackie Milburn, Vic Keeble and Bob Stokoe. Their supporters outnumbered the red ranks of York; the attendance of 65,000 remains, and is likely to forever remain, a record for a York match. As in the fifth round tie against Spurs, York fell behind early, to a Keeble goal. Bottom, almost inevitably, dragged them back into it on the half-hour. He dispossessed a Newcastle defender – either Stokoe or Scoular, depending on reports - on the halfway line, running unopposed to the edge of the penalty area before slotting it past the onrushing Simpson into an empty net.

There were no further goals, but there was considerable controversy. With ten minutes remaining, an almighty goalmouth scramble ended with Bottom heading what he thought was the winning goal, but Simpson clawed it back from - as many York supporters still maintain - behind the line.

The replay at Roker Park saw the Geordie giants eventually win through. Newcastle goals in the third and last minute bookended a spirited York performance, a 2-0 win for Newcastle sending them through to a final against Manchester City, which they won. This incredible York team became known as the Happy Wanderers, and they remain to this day one of a select band of third tier sides to make it all the way to an FA Cup semi-final, even if the ultimate fairytale ending just eluded them.

Mid-1990s League Cup wins over Manchester United and Everton, including a staggering 3-0 win at Old Trafford, further reinforced York's giant-killing reputation. For the time being, the FA Cup was the only way we could add to the list of scalps; six years have passed since we've been even allowed to enter the League Cup.

Back in 2009, two further home league games against Chester and Ebbsfleet provided a week off the bike and some time to kill in York. I spent some of it fixing up the bike, and some of it at the hospital visiting Gran, reminiscing with her about Grandad and his love of York City, their refereeing friend Lol Cousins, and Grandad's amateur playing days. She seemed in much better spirits. When we went through the usual rigmarole of saying that she'd soon be out, this time we both meant it.

I took a wrong turn on the way out of the hospital, ending up in a ward that faced towards Bootham Crescent. I was struck by a memory of having been in here overnight round about this time of year. In fact it was Bonfire Night. The 5th November is celebrated with extra gusto in York, as the city was Guy Fawkes' birthplace. I could remember hearing the bangs and crackles of fireworks mingled in with the shouts of the crowd. It was before I'd started going to watch York, but cooped up in my hospital bed, I was equally disappointed at missing out on the match and the rockets. I wondered whether my mind had conflated several different incidents, but a quick check in David Batters' brilliantly exhaustive *York City: The Complete Record* confirmed that we drew 1-1 at home to Torquay on 5th November 1988. I would have been in for either appendicitis or electrocution; they happened fairly close together.

York would go on to finish eleventh in the old Fourth Division that season, under the stewardship of two unremarkable managers in Bobby Saxton and John Bird. It had been a run-of-the-mill, bread-and-butter campaign. If you averaged out all of York's seasons; including seven which ended in re-election; taking into account the dark years down in the Conference; not forgetting the two glorious seasons in the old Second Division; and totting up all the others spent bobbing around the bottom two leagues, we'd probably end up about eleventh in the old Fourth Division. If not below.

Now, we were trying desperately to claw our way back to even that modest level. A midweek home match against bottom of the league Chester City offered a great way to keep the momentum going. Chester had started the campaign on minus twenty-five points and the club was now playing under the threat of expulsion from the league due to yet more financial mismanagement. Understandably, their form had suffered. The best they could hope for from this season would be to fulfil their fixtures and stave off liquidation. Relegation was already a certainty.

York started the match ruthlessly. Brodie trundled through the middle of a back-pedalling, parting defence to side-foot home after thirty seconds. On the half-hour he won yet another dubious penalty, falling to his knees like a stricken widow at the slightest of touches from behind. He converted it low and hard to the 'keeper's right. It took him all of two minutes of the second half to complete his first ever City hat-trick. Latching on to Lawless' through-ball, he wrong-footed centre back Kelly before thumping an emphatic curling finish from the edge of the box, across Danby into the bottom corner.

I was wrapped in a bear hug in the ensuing scrum. One of my best mates, Moll, had emigrated to Australia a few years before. He didn't get back to the UK often and when he did, he rarely had the time to make it out for a pint, let alone a match. We don't keep in touch as often as we should, and I'm by far the worst culprit. Moll's an Everton fan, but has watched York a fair few times over the years, without ever really supporting them. So, as fine as it was, the embrace was nothing really to do with Brodie's hat-trick goal. I hugged him back; it was great to see him.

At 3-0 down, Chester started to play with the shackles off. Anthony Barry reduced the deficit with an absolute peach of a thirty-yard strike. 'A brahmer', as my Dad next to me said. If indeed that's how you spell it. Deep into injury time he was given another chance to mutter about 'bloody Ingram', as the York 'keeper had once again made a characteristically uncharacteristic dash off his line to completely miss a free-kick and gift a free header to Kelly, who partially atoned for being bamboozled by Brodie by heading into Ingham's recently-vacated net. A second 3-2 win in four days, but this one felt much more routine. Another three points towards what was now plainly becoming a promotion attempt. Chester's players and fans were applauded off in a show of solidarity in their fight for survival. Like most clubs at this level and even one or two above, we'd been there.

'We could always nip into the Boot for one,' said Dad, pretending that the thought had just popped in to his head.

'Great idea. Anything to get out of this wind,' I replied, pretending that the suggestion was a surprise.

The Boot and Shoe is a lovely old low-slung pub which hums with the locals' constant chatter. It always seems busy, despite being tucked away on a dead-end road in a tiny village. It is a few short miles from the small market town of Pocklington, where Dad played most of his rugby. Many of his former teammates now get their sporting fix in a less bruising manner on the adjacent golf course at Aughton. We were bound to bump into one of them. This time it was Tim Slater. Due to Kev the landlord's generosity, it's usually difficult to pay for a beer. When Tim's holding court, it's downright impossible.

A couple of hours and several furiously quick pints later, we resumed our journeys; Dad returning to York with the wind at his back; me struggling into its teeth as far as I could get. After a few aimless miles I found myself in Howden. In order to inject some variety into the up-down-up-down monotony of following a northern team in a league with a heavy southern bias, I decided to cross the Humber Bridge, a pleasant side-effect of this choice being that I avoided Goole.

As I pottered along, I began to realise that today's ride with Dad, like the earlier ride into the Dales, had been a taster for the trip to Cambridge and back at the end of the month. He had been building up to doing a leg of the tour with me and we'd decided on the away league matches at Histon and Rushden. This out-and-back loop would take ten days or so. The Histon game had since been postponed due to our progress in the FA Cup. Drawing Cambridge out of the FA Cup hat had been a fortunate replacement fixture, as Histon is less than five miles to the north of the city.

The ride out with Dad to Ellerton had confirmed what we'd both known all along would form the pattern of the bigger trip. We would stop every twenty miles or so for a pint, we would bicker and whinge over shared characteristics, we would laugh at crap jokes, we would argue pedantically, we would suppress bigger grievances for the sake of continued companionship.

By the time I was watching the sun set, crawling along the magnificent bridge high above the Humber estuary, I was feeling pretty good about the choice of route. Dad would probably have already made it back home. I wondered if he was still thinking about the previous day's match with Ebbsfleet, the finer details of which I'd already forgotten. Another 1-0 home win, a Rankine tap in from a rare Dave McGurk shot. Three further points towards a hoped-for play-off place. A nothing game; one of many throughout the season. Home games have a tendency to merge into one; away matches always seem more memorable simply due to the fact that there's only one match played at each venue. And there was often new ground to cover in getting to the match, and a new ground as the destination.

Yes, watching the sun set from the bridge, I felt pretty happy with my lot. A few miles later, pedalling uphill in the dark into wind and rain, a certain amount of displeasure began to creep in. Isn't Lincolnshire supposed to be flat?

Over the previous week, large swathes of the country had been ravaged by south-westerly gales. I made it as far as Caistor before taking a room above a pub. The next day threw up more of the same lashing rain and cruel wind, the latter driving the former unerringly into my frozen face.

The bitter wind made me wonder if I'd ever make it to the next away match at AFC Wimbledon. I crawled up into the Lincolnshire Wolds and crept along an exposed road which had also formed part of the ancient, majestic Ridgeway I had struggled over twice on the Salisbury trip. This stretch inevitably took in the highest point in eastern England, which affords a fantastic view of the Wolds to both sides. At least that's what an information board said; I couldn't see a thing for the surrounding clouds, I could barely make out what was written on the board. The surrounding clouds began to empty themselves onto me and kept it up for the rest of the day.

Progress was horribly slow. Each fresh blast of wind seemed to make the panniers heavier. The blasts blew straight down my throat, with slight variations in direction providing little respite. I started to question my decision to ride towards the flattest, most exposed part of the country. Fortunately I had set off early from York, as I would need most of the week to get to London. A midweek match in the capital would have pushed me close to failing the challenge. By the time the winter postponements start to kick in, I will need to be served some large slices of luck to avoid such a fate.

Horncastle for lunch, Boston for tea, but no party. A forty-mile battle. I could nearly have walked it as quickly.

The Fenlands: otherworldly landscape of endless skies and eerie plains; flat-as-a-pancake reclaimed marshland and sea bed; isolated bolt-hole for wildlife and humans alike. As I crawled across the countryside, it was impossible not to be impressed with the latticework of ditches and canals, a testament to man's triumph over nature. The Fenlands' vast skies and widescreen horizons make for a truly striking and beautiful part of England, which is all the better for being sparsely populated and little-visited.

But it's a bloody horrible place to cycle when the wind's up. I was going to have three or four more days of this, at average speeds of up to some 7 (S E V E N) mph. I couldn't have made much slower progress cycling across an actual sea bed.

It was windy all over the country, but according to the locals I spoke to, this is a permanent feature in their corner of the world. How could you put up with this day after day? Surely it would send you slowly insane? I was sitting on a bench in Boston, reflecting on how the Pilgrim Fathers had probably had the right idea, when a man turned up to show me that even if the wind didn't necessarily bring about insanity, it could certainly make you a little *different*.

He approached my bike, which was propped up against the back of the bench. Lost in my thoughts, I only noticed him out of the corner of my eye, crouching on his haunches, rocking backwards and forwards and whistling to himself. The strangely hypnotic, rhythmic nature of his rocking suggested he'd been there for quite some time. I thought we were going to get into the usual conversation which is often struck up by a cycling enthusiast - what I'm up to, how they don't get out as often as they'd like, general bike chat about gear and clothing. Pleasant, everyday stuff. But the crouching man eschewed a humdrum greeting. After an uncomfortably long period spent whistling at my bike, he straightened himself up, tugged at his jacket lapels and barked, in a curious, wistful voice:

'Last time I went cycling, I were blown into a ditch.'

This was our whole conversation. He was scurrying off before I could muster a response, bent double into the merciless wind. I had little choice but to press on in his direction, at roughly his pace.

Thirty-odd miles further on, I got a bit lost in March. The town, not the month: I wasn't pedalling *quite* that slowly. I'd stopped for the night in Holbeach and had picked up a Sustrans cycle route a few miles into the day. The signposts and the trail both petered out in a wood, which was annoying but didn't faze me: waning signage seems to be a prominent feature of all their routes. I stopped an old boy coming the other way on his bike and asked for directions to the town centre.

After about fifteen seconds it became apparent that he a) had a quite appalling stutter and b) didn't have a fucking clue. It really was a spectacular stammer. I wouldn't be surprised to find he has an entry in the *Guinness Book of Records* under *Longest time spent giving erroneous directions*. We played out the rest of an *Open All Hours* out-take: the younger man on laden bike, the older guy spluttering ineffective instructions from beneath a bushy moustache. After an incredibly long time – at least two Boston bike whistles' worth - we came to the conclusion, by means of sign language and guesswork, that I should bear right at the end of the track. I thanked him and pedalled off, duly turning left at the end as the sign indicated.

Later that evening I rolled up at John's in Cambridge. The last few hours before I got there were amongst the worst I had spent since setting off in August. The gale blowing down my throat made the flattest part of the country feel like a constant steep climb. Even the smooth and commendable one-way system in Chatteris couldn't lift the gloom which had enveloped me. But John could.

Within a few minutes of walking through the door I was fed and watered, then ushered down to his local club for a couple of pints. The club's screen beamed back pictures from balmier climes. Malaga were entertaining Barcelona, whose silken assassins sliced through the home side's defence time after time.

John's hospitality continued in the morning with a full English breakfast. He even made me a packed lunch to set me on my way. We should probably marry.

Another day of small hills made big by the wind, icy rain and impotent whinging. I inched through Hare Street, Ware, Cheshunt and Enfield before snaking through London's outer north-western fringes to Ealing. I propped the bike against the wall of Will's strangely vast bathroom, where it would remain for a couple of days. I was glad to be off it.

On the morning of the match I met Russell, an AFC Wimbledon fan who had been in touch to offer to ride with me and to show me round the club on the day of the match. To Russell's disappointment, we met in Richmond. He'd been expecting a longer ride on the day but my early arrival in London had scuppered that.

'Sorry we're not going further today.'

'It's all right. I just thought you'd be coming in from Leicester or somewhere.'

I suppressed a laugh. There was no way I could cover so many miles before 3pm. Russell, in his late forties, in decent shape and a member of *Velo and Blue*, a Dons supporters' charity cycling club, probably could. We pushed on through a brick-pillared gate into Richmond Park.

'This is the away trip I've been most looking forward to. What you guys have created here out of nothing is really amazing. Sums up the Wimbledon spirit.'

'It's pretty amazing for us too. Eight years ago we were kicking ideas around in a pub, now we're one step away from being back in the Football League again. We never thought we'd do it this quickly.'

'Do you think the success is partly driven by anger at what happened?'

'Let's put it this way - when Franchise was given the go-ahead, I was angered, astonished and sad, like all of us were. I'd supported Wimbledon since 1966. The three-man commission that granted a franchise to Milton Keynes have a lot to answer for.'

That commission included the then York City chairman, Douglas Craig. A couple of months prior to being appointed to the commission which would decide Wimbledon's future, Craig had confirmed his intention to turf the club out of Bootham Crescent and sell the land to Persimmon Homes. This did not hinder his participation on the FA panel. Craig's heinous act can be seen as the first in a chain of calamitous events that led to our almost inevitable spell in non-league. But for the sterling efforts of the supporters, it could have been much worse. But I'll expand on our injustice later; this is the time to dwell on Wimbledon's.

The Crazy Gang's dizzying ascent from the Southern League to the First Division in just eight years is well-documented. This set of robust, roguish footballers wrote a tale even Roy of the Rovers' editors would have baulked at printing. The trip to the top table was capped off with an FA Cup win in 1988, which would become the club's high-water mark.

They hung on long enough at the highest level to become founder members of the Premier League. By this point they were ground-sharing with Crystal Palace at Selhurst Park. Wimbledon's notorious owner Sam Hammam had ten years previously slid the ownership of Plough Lane across to one of his own businesses. Two hundred miles north, Douglas Craig took eager notes. Perhaps with his forked tongue poking out of the corner of his mouth in concentration.

Semi-serious talk of a Wimbledon move to Dublin was quashed, first by the Football Association of Ireland, then by UEFA. Hammam had by this point sold out to some Norwegian powerboat enthusiasts. Charles Koppel bought the rest of Hammam's shares. Douglas Craig would do something remarkably similar, offloading York City to racing charlatan John Batchelor for a quid, whilst conveniently keeping Bootham Crescent for himself.

Dublin was replaced by Milton Keynes as a mooted venue for the club's new base. The ludicrous notion of shifting Wimbledon sixty-odd miles north somehow made it all the way through to the FA commission, who made their astonishing decision to allow the move to happen. To all but a handful of Wimbledon's fans, the new club was dead to them. Franchise FC had been born, with Douglas Craig a cooing midwife. Wimbledon's supporters resolved to overcome the enormous injustice of having their club stolen from them. AFC Wimbledon is the proof of their resolve.

Russell and I rounded a corner and saw the floodlights of Kingsmeadow. After buying me a fry-up in Fat Boys, the greasy spoon near AFC's current home, Russell walked us to the ground. He seemed to know everybody along the way, and introduced us to his fellow Wimbledon fans at every turn. One of them was Ivor Heller, a director of AFC Wimbledon, who Russell has known since they stood on the Plough Lane terraces together in the early 1970s. Ivor had been on Children in Need the night before, having raised thousands of pounds for the charity in the name of the club. Every single person who passed him stopped to say hello and to congratulate him. I got the feeling that this strength of togetherness was what pulled Wimbledon up through the leagues thirty years ago. You wouldn't bet against them doing it again.

The York fans had turned up in unusually good numbers; the turnstiles were overrun and the Wimbledon stewards were plainly unprepared.

'They reckoned you'd bring 200 to 250.'

There were clearly loads more than that. The large London exiles contingent was bolstered by hundreds more who'd made their way down from York. The City fans already in behind the goal were making a huge racket, chanting and banging the corrugated wall of the stand. The queue for the single open turnstile snaked from behind the goal round to the main stand. We less fortunates waited in line in the driving rain, missing the first fifteen minutes as a result.

We hadn't missed much, as the bucketing rain was making conditions difficult for both sides. It made for a dull spectacle. So dull that two of Adam's tag-along mates left at half-time. And they are Sheffield Wednesday fans. That's how poor it was. My old London flatmate Jo had been battling across town to make the match. She got to Kingsmeadow just in time to see the second half, which was a marginal improvement on the first. York's defence dominated throughout, with Ingham not called into action at all. Brodie and Rankine bullied the Wimbledon defenders with some excellent movement, but also some pretty hefty challenges and flying elbows. A robust attacking display if they're in your colours, a pair of dirty bastards if not.

Rankine got the only goal of the game just after the hour, diving through the rain to head in Chris Carruthers' excellent cross. About 800 York fans had squeezed in, and the few hundred with no roof over their heads danced a jig in the pouring rain. This sort of performance really seemed to suggest that we'd be making a sustained run at a play-off place. Scoring first and grimly hanging on was far from pretty to watch, but was proving damned effective for now.

In the packed bar afterwards, a sort of mini-variety performance was taking place. Compered by Ivor, people took it in turns to take the microphone, including Wimbledon's captain Paul Lorraine. He thanked the fans in a bashful way, and handed back to Ivor, who proceeded to draw a meat raffle. The whole thing was chaotic, low-key and a bit strange, but heartwarming: Phoenix Club Nights I suppose. We stayed a long time before carrying on the festivities in Kingston. I left the Kona behind the bar to collect the next day.

Ten hours later, I was picking my way through London's outer northern suburbs towards my internet blind date. At the start of the month, an email had appeared in my inbox entitled 'Fenland retreat'. Sam, a City fan exiled in Huntingdon, had seen an interview in *FourFourTwo* and offered me a bed and sustenance if I ever happened to be in the vicinity. Kind people who had only just met me had offered me a bed, sofa or tent pitch before, but this would be the first premeditated stay at a stranger's house. I was getting used to imposing myself on people I'd just met, but Sam must have been a bit twitchy about it. His girlfriend must have been terrified.

After St Albans came a series of towns whose names registered vaguely, like fragments of half-remembered songs or jokes. Wheathampstead, Hitchin, Henlow, Biggleswade, Gamlingay; all negotiated in gathering cold and gloom. By the time I skirted round the magnificently-named Papworth Everard I was nearly done for, but still had seven miles to go. They all seemed to be uphill. I arrived at Sam's a tired, sweaty mess. Despite this, he made me feel immediately at ease.

Over a beer we chatted about our respective City-supporting histories. Sam had had the good fortune to start going to Bootham Crescent a few years before I did, in the mid-1980s. His formative York-watching years included the all-conquering Fourth Division championship-winning season and the tilts at Arsenal and Liverpool in the FA Cup. I was fortunate enough to see the mid-1990s side in all its pomp, and naïve enough at the time to think that such success would continue. Those who started watching in the mid-to-late-1990s have never seen their side get promoted. There is an entire generation of York City fans who have only known failure and relegation. What if they never get to see a successful side? Keith Walwyn is Sam's hero. I still wax lyrical about Jon McCarthy and Paul Barnes. How are the fans who have only seen York fall through the leagues supposed to pass on their enthusiasm of Colin Alcide and Lee Nogan? The sooner we get out of this awful league the better.

After a couple more beers, Sam transported us back more than twenty years. He fished out a video cassette – video! – that a quick-thinking relative had recorded when a re-run of the Arsenal FA Cup match popped up on some channel or other. Having never seen it before, I was delighted. Sam has seen it hundreds of times, but still shared my delight. He handled the tape as a religious fanatic would handle a relic. With good reason: Sam's frequent viewings had left the tape scratchy and stretched almost to breaking point.

There didn't seem too much of a gulf in quality between the two sides, although the icy surface certainly helped the home team. Houchen seemed very young and remarkably calm before sticking away the decisive penalty. When the ball strikes the net, the camera pans back to take in the thousands of York fans tumbling joyously down the Shipton Street terracing. This part of the tape is as snowy as the touchlines; an eight-year-old Sam is in there somewhere but, despite years of forensic study, he's yet to spot himself.

The blind date had gone as well as it possibly could have, and Sam suggested we did the same again sometime soon. I shouldn't really have been worried; it wouldn't have been the trickiest of *Lonely Hearts* to write: *Mid-30s York City supporter, slightly thickening round the waist, fond of nights in with beer, pizza and re-runs of Houchen's winning penalty; WLTM similar for fun and friendship.*

A couple of days later I was back in York for another forgettable 1-0 win, the third in a row. The victory over Gateshead came courtesy of a Lawless header, his first goal for the club. The next day, Dad and I set off for our father-and-son tour. The Oedipedalers would take in the second round FA Cup match at Cambridge and the short hop across to the league game at Rushden & Diamonds a couple of days later, before returning north.

Part of me was happy for the company and for the chance to spend an extended period of time with Dad. On the other hand, I was worried for his physical health and concerned about what so much time in close proximity would do for our collective mental health. We made good initial progress, battling through a gale to spend the first night in Gainsborough. As a result of his accident, Dad was understandably nervous on the open road. We took cycle-paths whenever they were available and he would often ride on available footpaths alongside busier roads. I shielded him from the traffic where possible; it was one of the few times in my life I'd ever seen him scared.

It was my birthday at the end of the month and Dad had kindly offered to foot most of the bill for this leg as an extended birthday present. As a result, we slept in comfort, taming our thirst well each night. Time spent eating and digesting full English breakfasts and clearing fuzzy heads made for pleasingly late starts. Once on the road we pottered slowly along in convivial and conspiratorial spirits, stopping every couple of hours for a pint. It was a fine way to travel to Dad's first away match since the League Cup quarter-final against Rochdale in 1962, the year Dale made the final.

The last hour to John's in Cambridge took its toll on Dad's recently-healed legs. Wheezing up the hugely inconvenient hill just before John's house – the only one for miles around – I heard a soft sound from behind me like a crisp packet bursting underwater.

'Bugger!' That wet pop had come from Dad's knee. We walked the last few hundred metres. We had a couple of days rest between matches, but I wasn't sure that Dad would make it back to York.

His knee had recovered enough to make it to the Abbey Stadium the next day. Cambridge's ground is a proper ramshackle old stadium, similar to Bootham Crescent. Except they have flung up a lovely new stand at one end which is inexplicably given over to the away fans. From this excellent vantage point we witnessed a classic smash and grab raid. Cambridge were all over us for most of the match, forcing fifteen corners to our one. As the first half drew to a close, the tie was settled by two goals in as many minutes. For the opener, Rankine ambled forward before unleashing a fierce drive into the top corner from twenty-five yards. The ball arrowed towards the net from the moment of impact. Before the cheers, a momentary stunned pause. Rankine had never hinted at doing anything like this before; perhaps it hadn't happened. The pile of red shirts at the far end confirmed that we hadn't witnessed a mass *trompe l'oeil* – Rankine had pulled out an absolute belter which would rightly later be voted goal of the round. York supporters were still celebrating Rankine's thunderbolt when Brodie won a dodgy-looking penalty for a foul which seemed to take place outside of the box. He converted it low and hard to the 'keeper's right, doubling the undeserved lead.

Cambridge battered us for the whole of the second half, but the defence held firm until the eighty-fifth minute, when Tonkin clattered in a long-range effort off both posts. York survived a frenzied onslaught to take their place in the third round of the FA Cup for the first time in eight years. Friends old and new mingled in the brilliantly-named Dobblers pub to watch the third round draw. The ties would take place early in the New Year, immediately after an away match at Altrincham.

We watched and waited for ball sixty-one to be pulled out of the bag. *Please not Brighton away*. Sam and I were praying for Arsenal or Liverpool at the Crescent. *Please not Plymouth away*. Any top flight side would be good though. *Please not Portsmouth away*.

Stoke City. At their place. A crack at a top-flight side. A match we had little to no chance of winning but we would have a crack nonetheless. 'Could have been much worse' was the general consensus. It certainly could have been much worse for me. A short pedal down from Cheshire to the Potteries was in store, before a journey back to York for the next league match.

We went out to celebrate my birthday. A trip to a Premier League side had been secured, and six wins in a row. It had been some month.

DECEMBER

By Tuesday, Dad's knee was in good enough shape to attempt the forty-mile trip to the Rushden & Diamonds ground in Irthlingborough, where the resumption of league duties would see York attempting to win their seventh straight game to equal the record set by those Happy Wanderers of 1955. We flitted along foggy back roads, picking out red kites in the grey gloom. Even after stopping for a barely-earned pint at Grafham Water we pitched up in Rushden in the early afternoon.

We still had a few miles to go to get to the ground. Rushden & Diamonds was formed as an amalgamation of two clubs: Rushden Town and Irthlingborough Diamonds, with the merged club's ground situated in the latter town. After the 1992 merger, the new club gained a couple of quick promotions to find themselves in the Conference National. After a few more seasons at this level, finishing fourth, fourth and second, they eventually won the league to complete the rise from obscurity to the Football League. They got all the way to the play-off final in their inaugural season, where they lost to another former non-league side, Cheltenham Town. But promotion to the third tier was secured at the second attempt, the Northamptonshire side winning the league title on the last weekend of the season.

Theirs had been a heady rise from the seventh to third step of the pyramid in a little over ten years from formation. The descent has been equally sharp. Max Griggs, the Dr. Martens owner who masterminded the merger and bankrolled the success, pulled out and handed the club over to the supporters. The club quickly found itself back in the Conference, beset by financial problems. Despite their off-field woes, they were having an incongruously successful season this time round. In good form coming into the match against York, if they kept it up they would be challenging alongside us for a play-off place.

We rolled into Irthlingborough and went to the ground early before finding somewhere to stay. We found Nene Park easily enough, lurking as it was on the edge of an industrial estate next to the eponymous river. It's a neat little ground, much less generic than the usual identikit new-builds. We took photos as proof of our arrival then grimaced our way up the hill into town. A welcoming pub, the Oliver Twist, agreed to put us up for the night, so we stowed the bikes in the stables and took a pint, moderately-earned this time. Sam had made the short trip across from Huntingdon, so we took a stroll down the hill to the next pub to meet him. He'd brought a mate with him, a friendly motormouth

Mackem by the name of John Hindhaugh. He drank quickly and spoke quicker. It came as no surprise to hear that he was a motorsport commentator: he could talk the Hindhaugh legs off a donkey. Over his second rapid pint he promised to provide a running commentary throughout the game. Long since having given up on joining in the conversation, none of us doubted he could.

Nothing much went on in the first half. Even John's promised commentary petered out towards half-time. Midway through the second half, James Meredith foraged up the wing from his left back berth to force a corner. Brodie produced an other-worldly charge into the box, leaving his markers looking like mere Irthlings, to nod in Barrett's inswinging delivery.

As in previous matches, Foyle's men opted to defend the slender lead rather than try to incite anything approaching fervour in the away crowd. It was soporific to watch, but effective. Seven wins in a row, all by one-goal margins. Amongst this procession of tight victories, only the Cup match against Crewe had really set the pulse racing. Were we going to bore our way to the play-offs?

Sando was certainly starting to think so.

'I've started pricing up bikes. I'm thinking of getting a hybrid so after we've done I can commute on it from time to time.' This from the man who hadn't turned a pedal in anger for twenty-five years.

'Sounds sensible. You should get something half-decent for £400 or so.'

He gave a rueful shake of the head. 'It's not just that though, Simon - there's the clothing. And some shoes. And a tent. It's going to cost me a bloody fortune all this success.'

After breakfast, Dad declared himself match fit for the trip back north. His knee was immediately tested by a couple of surprisingly vicious climbs that brought us to Oundle, a pleasant, slightly austere-looking market town and home of the renowned private school. A few miles further on, we rolled through the village of Fotheringhay, where our thin veneer of pure camaraderie began to be partially rubbed away.

Dad offered up a history lesson. 'Dick Three was born here. And it was round here that Mary Queen of Scots had her head lopped off I think.'

'I know.'

'How come you know? I thought you took no interest in History.'

'Because I just read it off the same sign you did.' *He knows I'm interested in history.*

'What sign?' His faux-naïve question was accompanied by a series of barely-believable *'What? Me?'* shrugs.

'Come on, your eyesight's not that bad.' And for the sake of the rest of the trip, I left it at that. At least I should have done.

'Why do you always do this?'

'Do what? I've no idea what you're on about.' This time his protestations seemed more genuine.

'Pass off very recently-acquired knowledge as long-held. It's OK to not know stuff, otherwise how do you ever learn anything?'

'I didn't realise I did that. I don't know why it bothers you so much.'

'I *don't* know why it bothers me so much either.'

I don't know why, it just does. Pathetic really. I'm pathetic. He's pathetic. We're pathetic. We pedalled on, pathetically.

We struggled to make fifty miles that day. Northamptonshire was surprisingly hilly and Leicestershire offered little respite. Although he would never admit it, I think that Dad was starting to suffer from several days' consecutive exercise, and he hadn't really recovered from his knee nearly giving way a couple of days before. This all made for slow going. By the time we'd struggled up and giddily descended one of the seemingly interminable hills which surround and protect Grantham, we decided to call it quits for the day. It was too dark to see but I knew that Grantham lies at the bottom of a bowl and that we would have a similar climb to start the next day. I kept that to myself while we found a B&B. After checking in we found a quirky little pub, the self-deprecatingly named Nobody Inn, which was selling good local ale.

Over the second pint I received the phone call I'd been dreading. Well, I missed the call and picked up Mum's normal – far too normal – voicemail when we were traipsing round the adjacent Asda buying a roast chicken and cheap red wine dinner. I was to ring her back when I got the chance. Back at the B&B I poured myself a glass of wine from the bottle we'd just bought, downed it and went outside to make a call that I didn't want to put either of us through.

Mum's calmness put both of us at ease. She was as well as she could be, and had other family around. No, there was nothing I could do; it would all be taken care of. In fact, most of it already had been. She preferred to keep herself busy. I wasn't to worry about not being there, my brother and sister were away from York too. No, I needn't get the train back; I should just treat the cycling as my job and make it back to York as normal. It's what Gran would have wanted me to do. I'd be back in time for the funeral.

All this time on my own on the bike had given me plenty of scope for contemplation, which had naturally recently centred on Gran. She had had a good, long life full of laughter. She had devoted herself to her husband and family and was universally adored as a result. She had the rare knack of making all those around her feel at ease and in good spirits. I thought about the fact that Gran had died while I was in Grantham; against my will my mind idly considered a pun or two. Gran would have approved. She would certainly have enjoyed the minor coincidence. Canny, she would have said. You wouldn't credit it.

I had a bit of a cry, strolled up and down the High Street, called Jola to tell her the news and, at a loss, wandered back to the B&B.

I opened the door to find the walls at Dad's side of the room stained red up to a height of eighteen inches or so. It looked like he'd murdered a midget. Or a tall cat.

'Have I caught you mid-sacrifice?'

'I had a few issues with the bottle. It was somewhat recalcitrant. Is Bid a goner, then?'

I was angry at his insensitivity. Fucking livid. But, being English, and already emotionally drained, decided not to rise to it. He'd known Gran for thirty-five years. They'd always got on really well; I thought he would have been more upset. Perhaps he was. Maybe this was just his way of dealing with it.

I knocked back what wine I could salvage. 'Yes. I'm off to sleep.'

It took us a further two days to get back to York. Little by little, the sense of camaraderie seeped back in. On the whole, it had been great to spend this much time together again. We would always bicker; we're much more similar in personality than either of us would care to admit. The good spirits and bonhomie had well outweighed the sniping. Doing something demanding in close proximity was always going to lead to pressure building up between us, and it was relieved as naturally as a storm sweeping away prolonged humidity. We hadn't fallen out properly, so the trip had to be classed as a success. And I was genuinely grateful of the extended birthday present of Dad footing the bill for the entire leg of the tour.

Given the fact that he'd broken most of the bones in his body a few short years previously, he had done astonishingly well to see the journey out – we'd covered more than 350 miles over ten days, but only eight of those days were spent in the saddle. Nearly fifty miles a day for a man who'd recently spent a month in a coma. And he had had to put up with me. Impressive stuff: I told him so. He shrugged it off in the same dispassionate way he'd shrugged off Gran's death. Stuff matters less since his accident. We parted at Naburn, the village where I went to primary school and where the York-Selby bike track crosses the Ouse. He made for home; I turned my attention to Bishopthorpe and my Mum.

York 2 Wrexham 1. Some matches this season had been half-forgotten, but I genuinely can't remember anything about this one. I definitely went, but I took no notes. In fairness, I was preoccupied. Family was more important than football. So I've had to resort to match reports to get anything down on paper. Apparently Chris Carruthers got forward sufficiently to head his first goal for the club after only six minutes. Late on, Brodie nodded in Lawless' rebounded shot to double our lead. His twentieth goal of the season already – the quickest that any York player has ever reached this landmark. Curtis Obeng pulled one back for Wrexham shortly afterwards, but York rode out the remaining few minutes to claim yet another victory. Eight in a row now to match the Happy Wanderers' 1955 run; this was heady stuff.

At least you'd think so. In truth, Foyle's brand of ultra-functional football made the continued success less enjoyable than it ought to have been. Also, despite the amazing run, we were treading water in the league. Oxford still imperiously headed the table, and Stevenage were chugging along menacingly in second place. We were solidly entrenched in the play-off positions, but a title challenge seemed highly unlikely.

The FA Trophy, non-league's premier knock-out competition, is looked down on by most of our fans. Despite the six years we've languished down here, we don't really see ourselves as a non-league club and consequently the Trophy is sneeringly seen as beneath us. I usually agree wholeheartedly with this kind of baseless superiority, but this season's FA Trophy would bring welcome respite in the form of a week off the bike. One of the ground rules I had arbitrarily laid down was that I wouldn't pedal to Trophy matches. The club takes the tournament much more seriously than the fans do, so we ran the risk of a lengthy run. This would heap further pressure on an already overloaded fixture list, creaking as it would be with rearranged matches called off for heavy or frozen pitches. So I benched myself for the Trophy run.

Missing out on the glamour of a trip to Hinckley was my punishment. No 200 mile round trip in awful weather to witness a 0-0 draw. A real sickener, but I took it in my stride as best as I could. The subsequent replay meant that the away match at Grays Athletic in deepest Essex was nudged a week closer to Christmas. I set off for it in sleety, blustery weather after a week of doing nothing. For the first time, what I was doing felt a bit futile. What was I doing pedalling 200 miles into the wind, under grey skies and in the dark, towards a nothing town on the Thames Estuary, to watch a poor-quality football match in a crumbling little ground in which the away supporters would outnumber the home following? I couldn't come up with many reasons as to why, but I turned the pedals all the same. The weather worsened as I got further south. Remaining upright, rather than making miles, became the priority. The snow fell hard and froze overnight. I fell frequently. It's fair to say this leg was a low point of the trip.

Over a leisurely breakfast at Will's on the morning of the match, the first news of a pitch inspection started to filter through. Grays' official website remained upbeat, calling for supporters with 'small tractors or quad bikes' to make their way down to the ground to clear the snow off the pitch. A niche appeal, especially in urban Essex. At 11am the pitch was deemed playable. At 12pm they weren't so sure. I couldn't leave it any later so I set off for the dash across town from Ealing.

I'd only made it as far as Acton before it became painfully obvious that I would fail to make kick off, and thus fail the challenge. The elasticated strap that held all the gear on top of the panniers together pinged off straight into the chainset, where it wedged itself. The sharp stop caused me to fall onto the pavement, to the pedestrians' annoyance. They could at least have laughed. A quick search of my bags revealed that I had indeed left all of my tools in York. If you ever find yourself in a similar situation, here's a timesaving tip: a biro and a plastic fork will not do the job.

I walked a couple of miles to the nearest bike shop where they fixed it in less than a minute with a tool remarkably similar to the one I could picture on the kitchen worktop at Dad's. I'd wasted so much time that I rang Will and told him to wait while I tucked my tail between my legs and pedalled back to his.

At 1pm, the referee deemed the surface definitely fit for use. The match would go ahead and I would fail. We took the tube to Liverpool Street together. We surfaced to change trains, to find that at 1.15pm the referee realised she'd made an enormous mistake and reversed her decision, calling the match off.

Hang on.

If I'd cycled most of the way to an abandoned match, then it didn't really matter that I'd missed a few miles out did it? I'd be pedalling to and from the rearranged fixture anyway. I'd set out to get to every league and FA Cup match and back. If the game was postponed, then it didn't count as a real fixture, surely? These were extra miles, if anything. I'd gone above and beyond. Christ, I was awesome. I thought I was off the hook. I decided to check with the severest of my critics.

'Will?'

'Wha-aat?' He drew the word out into two syllables, in the way he does when I'm about to ask him to do something he thinks he doesn't want to do.

'Am I off the hook?'

'Do you know what? I think you are, you spawny twat.'

I handed him his pint. 'Good. I suppose now's as good a time as any to tell you about the train I got.'

'You what?' He spluttered beer froth all over his splendid moustache.

'Yeah, I kept getting punctures yesterday. Two before I'd even left Huntingdon, then a couple more along the way. I ran out of puncture repair stuff, and used all my good inner tubes up so had to resort to some crappy ones I'd bought in Newark. They kept tearing at the valve.'

I took a good swig of the festive ale that I'd chosen, having been predictably goaded into its purchase by the flashing LED on the pump clip that periodically lit up Rudolph's nose.

'Awful that, isn't it?'

Will nodded his agreement. 'Hideous. Carry on.'

'I looked for the nearest bike shop on my phone, but it was miles away. So I tried hitching to Hitchin.'

'Stop it.'

'Honestly. But nobody wanted to stop for the sweaty, hairy snowman. So I walked to Sandy and got the train. Nice name for a town isn't it?'

'You cheating twat.'

'Not really, I figured I'd go back and make the miles up later on.' I took another brave swig of Rudolph's Piss. 'But now I don't have to.'

'You spawny twat.'

'I've cycled 200 miles to get here.'

'Cycled some of it, you tart.'

'I've cycled *nearly* 200 miles to watch a phantom football match, now I have to pedal all the way back home in ice and snow for Christmas. And I've got to do all this again for the rearranged game. Only you could suggest that's lucky.'

We were swallowed up by the greater group, which included a yet-more-resigned-to-his-fate Sando. The Square Mile pub was almost completely taken over by happily festive York City fans, a pre-Christmas swarm of red and blue toasting a match that never was.

In the morning, I weighed up the rules of my challenge and whether they meant that I had to cycle back to York or not. Even Will agreed that, strictly speaking, I didn't have to. But I had to get back somehow and cycling seemed the most obvious and cheapest way, and certainly the most natural. Cycling was just what I did now. So I decided to pedal back. At the very least I'd have the extra miles in the bank to play with in case of future fixture problems. A Brodie hat-trick in the FA Trophy replay against Hinckley three days earlier had all but assured that eventuality.

All moral wrangling went out of the window within a minute of leaving Will's flat. As I turned to negotiate the T-junction, my wheels went from under me, sending my shoulder and knee crunching into the ice-clad tarmac. I hadn't even made it out of Will's road. The bike was useless in these conditions. I'd definitely have been better off on a small tractor or a quad bike. Maybe I should have put out an appeal.

Convincing myself that I'd not actually missed a match, and that I'd be pedalling back for the rearranged fixture, I walked gingerly back to Will's. I wasn't about to kill myself slipping and sliding back from a postponed fixture. A cup of calming sugary tea later, we'd agreed that I'd leave the Ridgeback in his bathroom for a while; I'd be coaxing the whimsical Kona out of hiding again. Will and I bid each other all the festive best and I took the coach home for Christmas.

Considering Jola was in attendance, the Boxing Day match against Mansfield Town went surprisingly smoothly. The Nottinghamshire side were sitting in sixth place, just outside the playoffs, and were expected to provide a tough test of our promotion credentials. In reality, they were brushed aside fairly easily. The teams ran out in front of a bumper crowd of more than 4,500, with 650 or so from Mansfield. The York ranks were swollen by the regulars' friends and family tagging along for their one game of the season.

York controlled the game throughout. Brodie inevitably opened the scoring after twenty minutes, heading in Luke Graham's flick-on from a yard out. Graham had become an integral part of the team since his loan move from Mansfield, and the defence had become an even tighter unit with him at the centre of it alongside McGurk. An unruffled presence at centre back, he reads the game well and seems to never miss a header. It had been a strange move by the Stags to let him go on loan, compounded by the decision to let him play against them.

Straight after half time, Lawless slipped a great ball through for Brodie to gallop on to. Another hasty challenge, another theatrical tumble, another defender red carded, another penalty won. He converted it low and hard to the 'keeper's right. The ten remaining Stags contained us for most of the rest of the match, but with ten minutes left Michael Gash came off the bench and marked his return from injury by scoring with his first touch to complete an emphatic 3-0 win. All of a sudden we were only seven points behind an Oxford side that had previously seemed uncatchable. A win at Altrincham in a couple of days' time and we'd really be breathing down their necks.

The matches over the festive period had fallen pretty well for those of us cycling to every match. The trip over the snowy Pennines would be followed by a short spin down to Stoke for the FA Cup third round tie on 2nd January. I intended to get down there straight after the Alty match to bag the ground early, then hop on a train to Derby to spend New Year with my sister's family. The next round of the FA Trophy meant that after the Stoke game I had ten days or so off the bike, so Jola and I were going to fly to Poland for a short break.

But before Wrocław, Altrincham. There was no time to spare, so I spent some of Boxing Day night shivering along the B1224 to my brother Paul's house in Wetherby. The following morning was freezing, but crisp and clear. I took the stunning route out past Harewood House, through Pool and along Wharfedale to handsome, solid, dependable Otley. After flirting dangerously with Bingley's outskirts, the Kona and I battled through the moors and onto the tops.

It was already dark, and a frost had descended with the night. My hands were numb from the cold despite two pairs of gloves. Glacial fingers of wind slipped under my scarf, ruffled my hair through my helmet and tightened round my throat. Twice on the climb up to Brow Top the wheels slid abruptly from under me, leaving me howling obscenities at the near-full moon from the snow-piled verge. There hadn't been such a public display of madness round here since Branwell Brontë last overdid the laudanum. Between us, the Kona and I had conjured a performance that gave a whole new meaning to *out on the wiley, windy moors we'd roll and fall in green.*

Eventually, we – the Kona and I - crested Brow Top to be met with a glistening panorama of virginal white hills. In a fold below, Haworth's electric lights burnt yolk yellow against the snow. I toyed with stopping there for the night, but reasoned that it would leave too much to do the next day. Also, now I was up on the tops, I felt invigorated and wanted to pedal on into all that freshness. Humiliating falls and biting cold aside, this had been one of the finest days of the whole trip. Up here the sharp winter air tasted pure, the snow-covered moors dazzled bright enough to break out the shades and the roads were empty: no other bugger was stupid enough to be out in this, even in a car. Once again I remembered how lucky I was to be doing what I was doing. And I still had four whole months of this left. Then it struck me that we were already well past the season's mid-point. I only had four months of this left. I held that thought, and the brake levers, all the way to Hebden Bridge.

'I take it you've heard?' A call from Will's brother, Stu.

'No, not yet. So it's off then?'

'Ref deemed it unplayable just now. Sounds iffy – apparently there are only a couple of patches of snow in the six-yard boxes and the centre circle.'

'They're made of less stern stuff this side of the Pennines.' A legion of York fans had worked off the Christmas turkey clearing a heap of snow off the pitch before the Mansfield match, even enlisting the referee to the cause.

'True. It's not as if Alty even use the centre circle.'

'Haha! Thanks for letting me know, Stu. I'm in Rochdale – until your call I genuinely didn't think things could get any worse.'

'Happy to help. So now what?'

'I'm gonna head to the ground anyway. You never know when the rearrangement will be – might be a day after Eastbourne away. Then I'm off for a pint. You coming to Stoke?'

'No, I'm working. I'll see you for the Hayes game.' Stu is the sports editor of the local York press, the imaginatively-titled *The Press*, so often has to work when City are playing, to pull the next day's edition together.

I cut across Manchester to Moss Lane, home of Altrincham FC. It was disappointing that the match had been cancelled as York would have brought a lot of fans to the homely little ground. A proper atmosphere is hard to come by these days, and I'm pretty sure this would have been up there with the Wimbledon trip this season. But now it would be rescheduled for a Tuesday night sometime, instead of the Saturday between Christmas and New Year, and we'd bring a lot fewer fans as a result. There was nobody at the ground. I propped my bike up next to the silent turnstiles, beneath a match poster which had had a 'POSTPONED' sticker splashed across it at an unacceptably jaunty angle, took a photo for posterity and started picking my way back across the south of Manchester.

A night out in Chorlton with my old University flatmate Matilda led to a late start the next day. The road past the airport led to Wilmslow and Alderley Edge, villages dotted with footballers' houses and eye-wateringly expensive boutiques. I trundled on through Congleton and Kidsgrove and pitched up in Stoke-on-Trent in the mid-afternoon. After some misdirection I found the Britannia, squatting like many newly-built stadia on the corner of a trading estate. Like Stoke, it was a crushingly desolate place, surrounded by empty car parks and equally empty Harvesters. Harrowing. The wind screeched infernally off the surrounding steel, as if the Tin Man's new-found heart were being torn to shreds. What remains after the apocalypse will look and sound an awful lot like the Britannia Stadium on a non-match day.

I'd come here deliberately early so that I didn't have to spend New Year's Day getting to Manchester to resume the trip to Stoke. Two empty grounds in a row, snared early for different reasons. I hoped to be able to make it to Altrincham for the rearranged match, and in all likelihood would be able to. I had nothing against doing the extra miles, in fact I enjoyed being on the bike, but making it to the ground for the postponed match had given me some insurance in case things went awry. I pedalled back to the station and boarded a train to Derby, experiencing for the third time that month the illicit thrill of public transport.

JANUARY

Fat snowflakes slid down the outside of the Harvester's windows. Inside, they began to be obscured by steam. The place was packed with a good mix of fans trading chants; prosaic strains of *We Are York* battled for pub supremacy with the much less commonplace *Delilah*. Amidst the tribal singing, rumours began to circulate that the York team coach had been delayed. A text from my Dad, who was travelling across on one of the many supporters' coaches: *Stuck.* I'm pretty sure he thinks texts are charged by the character.

Adam and my real Uncle Graham arrived to confirm the rumours: they'd heard on the radio that the team and many fans had been held up by a mixture of snow and traffic on the M62. The M62?! The country, especially the North, had been covered in snow for weeks, with more not only expected but almost guaranteed. So why choose to take the highest motorway in the land, why not down the M1 and across? Why not come down the night before? A strange couple of decisions which might ultimately have cost us the match without a ball being kicked. More murmurings: if York didn't get to the ground by 3pm, they would forfeit the match.

Not the best preparation for the biggest match of the season. No non-league side had knocked out top-flight opposition since Sutton United beat Coventry City 2-1 in 1989. It felt strange to think of the gulf between York and Stoke in the same terms: this had been a league fixture as recently as 1999. But the harsh reality was that we were in the Conference, as Sutton had been, and we had very little chance of repeating their feat. Stoke were in mid-table in the Premier League, with a solid home record. Our recent run of form had got a fair few people dreaming – *if we can bring them back to the Crescent then you never know* - but hardly anyone gave us a serious chance of causing an upset.

The team coach drew up at the Britannia at 2.59pm. The match *would* kick-off, with a half-hour delay. Many York fans were still to arrive, including those on the coach my Dad was on. Further terse missives suggested that he would be unlikely to make it to the ground for kick-off. I felt really bad about this, not least because he had my ticket.

Someone bought another round. The clock ticked round to 3.15pm. I rang Dad. No answer. Texted him. No reply. Steve was travelling with him. Straight to voicemail. They must be out of range. I had no idea how much longer they'd be; if they'd even make kick-off. Everyone else in our group had their own tickets; I was the only one this disorganised. I decided to blag it.

The stadium and its environs were much cheerier on a match day. Crowd noise reverberated back from the surrounding metal, rather than the desolate wind. The streets were crowded with people rushing to make the delayed kick-off. I rushed along with them to the main entrance, had a word with a steward who had a word with someone else, who did the same. Thanks to the Stoke City staff's amenability, within five minutes flat I was heading up the stairs to the top tier with a press pass round my neck. As I was cantering upwards, I received another text from my Dad: *Police escort*.

Wondering what he'd done this time, I walked out into the stand and found a spare seat next to a middle-aged *Yorkshire Post* journalist who was covering York for the first time – a measure of how far we've fallen and for how long. When we were in the league the *Yorkshire Post* would report on each match, but now only turned up for the rare big occasions like today. Two doors down was Max Benson, an excellent student journalist who writes the match reports for the official York City website. Each of us had a small flatscreen TV bolted to the desk in front of us, which seemed to serve no purpose other than to relay a smaller version of the action you could see with your own eyes.

The pitch looked fantastic, an iridescent green advertisement for its undersoil heating. The home stands were sprinkled with fans throughout, probably half full. To our right, the away end was packed. We must have brought about 5,000. Dad's coach must have been one of the unluckiest, as there were hardly any spare seats left in the stand. I was scanning the snowy hills behind the York end when a blue flash caught the corner of my eye. A couple of Police vans were leading a mini-convoy of York supporters' coaches up the road adjacent to the stadium and into the car park behind the stand. The teams had only just run out onto the pitch; Dad and Steve had made it.

Stoke started the match well, with Ricardo Fuller's trickery and Matthew Etherington's direct running causing our centre backs all kinds of problems. But their early dominance failed to yield an opening goal and we started to get more into the game, mainly thanks to Barrett and Mackin in midfield, who did not look at all outclassed. The gulf in class was more apparent further upfield, where Brodie and Rankine were constantly stymied by the superior ability of Stoke's centre backs. Midway through the first half, Brodie tumbled under a Robert Huth challenge just outside the area. Barrett rose to meet the resulting free-kick from Lawless, casually flicking it into the far corner of Sorensen's net. A momentary pause of stunned disbelief gave way to pandemonium in the away end. Max and I hugged like reunited wartime sweethearts and danced around the press box. Not the done thing, judging by the Yorkshire Post man's sniffy reaction to being caught up in it.

We had barely had time to disentangle ourselves from him before the hosts equalised. A Delap throw – what else? – led to mass confusion in the York box. Danny Parslow took it upon himself to clear the danger with a hideous slice into his own net. Within a few seconds, Stoke's well-documented main danger had struck again. Another hurled missile wreaked havoc in the area. Only Fuller kept his head in the ensuing scrum, poking home from a yard or two out. We were neither the first nor the best side to be undone by Delap's long throws, but it felt especially cruel that our ephemeral euphoria should be ended by a passage of play so grimly predictable.

I rejoined the rest of my group at half-time. Dad and Steve hadn't missed a kick. The general feeling was that we hadn't been totally outclassed. And at 2-1 we weren't out of it. *If we can just bring them back to the Crescent...*

A well-taken Etherington free kick just before the hour killed off any hope of that. Shortly afterwards, Tuncay replaced a largely ineffective James Beattie. We brought on Kevin Gall. Despite the obvious difference in ability and available talent, we had been far from embarrassed. The midfield had more than held its own, and the fantastic travelling support had outsung the much-heralded loudest-in-the-Premier-League home fans: the York fans had been much the louder even when I was listening from my first-half eyrie surrounded by Stoke supporters.

There were no real what-might-have-beens. We had been beaten by the better, more muscular side, but shown real promise in the process. This York team should really be making the play-offs.

Having heard the predictable news that the rearranged Altrincham away match had again been called off, we flew to Poland. I had been prepared to pedal from Stoke to Cheshire, but hadn't really expected to have to do so. With more adverse weather to come, the match wouldn't be staged any time soon. With the FA Trophy once again taking centre stage, the next scheduled league game wasn't until the 16th January, which meant I had nothing to do for a couple of weeks.

I hitched from Derby to Luton Airport, met Jola and booked into a hotel for a couple of days until the snowstorms cleared sufficiently to allow take-off. Once in her stunning home town of Wrocław we mooched about as tourists; met up with friends for Zywiec and Zubrówka in the numerous bars which are hidden away down side-streets off the magnificent main square, Rynek; ate her Mum's incredible homemade food; listened bemused to me being interviewed on English-language Polish radio. Not half as bemused as their regular listeners, I'd imagine.

We visited Jola's uncle Stefan, whose English is even more basic than my Polish. Stefan and I meet once or twice a year. He plies me with gin and tonic and he beats me at chess. Not that he needs to do the former to achieve the latter. He and I ended up alone in the sitting room, which was dominated by a recently-acquired table football table. He poured us both a large gin and tonic. *Na zdrowie.* With the G&T as one prop and the *babyfoot* for another, our lack of shared language no longer seemed to matter as much. No different from men the world over who *do* speak the same language: emotional cripples held up by the wonderful, comforting crutches of booze and sport.

Pierre Littbarski would be my lynchpin. Partly because he'd drifted into the middle of a crowded midfield from his usual place on the wing, but mainly because his was the only name I could make out on the back of the shirts. I assumed I was 1980s West Germany, purely on the basis of that one legible name. We were in York City red. Strange, because traditional German white wouldn't have clashed with the opposition's blue. I had a black guy at centre forward, although Littbarski and Gerald Asamoah could never have played in the same team. I had no idea who he was supposed to be. There were no facial clues, as both he and the opposition goalie had been decapitated. I'd chip that stunted 'keeper before the game was out. Reparation for all those checkmates.

Stefan leant across the table to shake hands, averting his gaze as always at the point of contact. He is a tall, thin man with quick, darting eyes and a fine-featured face. Good bone structure, even if those bones are a little too close to the surface. An intimidating presence across the chess board, where he delights in mercilessly pulling apart my flimsy game, but I was pretty sure I'd get the better of him here. His introspective Slavic soul is more suited to whispering death in a king's ear than to the crude fury of table football.

'The very best of luck.' He has a pleasant voice, if a little thin. I was guessing at his words. It seemed the sort of thing that one ought to say in this situation, and Stefan is an earnest, formal sort of man.

'Good.' I couldn't remember the word for luck, even though I thought he'd just said it. Instead of making a spluttering attempt at it, I smiled and nodded my head and withdrew my hand from his. We both took a quick, deep pull from our gin and tonics. Stefan reached into the space behind his goal to retrieve a ball. *Won't be the last time you do that, mate.* He slipped it through the hole in the middle and we were off. The ball dropped straight to Littbarski, who threaded it expertly through to Not Asamoah, who placed it calmly to the left of the headless goalie: Albert Camus, I guess. 1–0. The blue stooges hadn't even touched the ball yet. *Think of that next time you imperil my queen with your rook/knight combo.* Stefan picked the ball out again, winced at me and dropped it back into play.

Without wishing to boast, I am a good player. I'm terrible at all manner of things, chess being one of them. But I am a good table football player. I learnt to play when I was very young on a Formica-clad table in our garage. Rows of red and yellow players strung out in that dashingly cavalier 2-5-3 formation. Enough to give Martin Foyle a seizure. My brother Paul, then a Liverpool fan (yes, he switched allegiance. Not only that, but to Leeds!) saw to it that I was always yellow. It wasn't long before I was making a mockery of our eight-year age gap, thrashing the ball past Clemence with unabashed glee. I honed my skills on family holidays in France, crowding round the table with the local boys, my sun-tinged English face a pink buoy in an olive sea. Their control mesmerised me. Standing on the ball; tippy-tappy passes; one-twos off the wall; pinpoint shots from defence; all tricks I copied when I got back home. Tricks I was now using to batter Stefan into submission.

'What's the score?' Stefan's wife Ella had wandered in from the kitchen to watch. Ella had bought the table across the border in Germany, the previous owner having presumably painted on the names. I was glad she had, it made a welcome change from being drubbed across the chequerboard. Stefan and I have probably shared more games of chess, and certainly more gins, than we have words. This is an agreeable arrangement for us both, and we like each other.

'Yes, what's the score?' Stefan echoed. *Why don't you check, mate?*

'Nine zero.' I didn't know the word for nil. I nudged the ball forward with my 'keeper, who was resplendent with a head, to the left back. He flicked it first time to Littbarski, who spotted a gap in the busy midfield and drilled it low and hard to Camus' right. He stood as immobile as my king usually does. 10-0.

'Another?' I knew the shorthand; it meant both game and gin.

'Yes, why not?' I would go easier this time, but still win. An orange ball was produced from behind the goal.

'Because of snow, yes?' I don't know how to say '*outside*' and he made no attempt to understand. I was toying with the idea of sprinkling icing sugar or similar on the pitch, to demonstrate the meteorological conditions under which an orange ball would be brought into play, when Stefan netted his first goal. We toed-and-froed, the game became bogged down. The midfield danced; half can-can, half haka. We were as entrenched as WWI soldiers, and made as much headway. I toyed with him a while, let him think he might win, before pulling pitilessly ahead. Harsh, you may think, but then you've not experienced his unblinking pitiless eyes boring into you whilst you dither over the precise square on which to sacrifice your bishop.

'Six four.' A third game. It would be the last. I once saw a French teenager chip the ball. My only goal in this match was to replicate his youthful, arrogant skill; to impart enough spin on the ball to loft it over Camus' headless shoulders and in. It was more difficult than I imagined it might be. I sliced repeatedly wide, missed the ball completely, stood on it and hurt my wrist. Stefan plundered goal after goal. He went 9-0 up.

Littbarski picked out Not Asamoah for the umpteenth time. A vicious downward stab caused the table to indent. The ball arced upwards, briefly granting Camus an orange face before it dropped behind his back and rolled into the net. Success.

'Nine one. Good played.' I offered my hand.

'Another?'

'Gin yes, football no. Chess?'

The table football matches took place on 7th January 2010. Exactly eight years before, more than 300 people had packed into Tempest Anderson Hall in York for a hastily-convened supporters' meeting. The previous month had seen incumbent York City chairman Douglas Craig make the abrupt, stark statement that '*at the end of the season the board of York City Football Club intend to resign and, in the interim, invite anyone interested in acquiring the football club to write to the chairman to obtain further details'*. If nobody came forward he would withdraw the club from the League. The meeting was for supporters to work out how exactly to save their club from dying a swift death.

In taking over from the well-liked Michael Sinclair, Douglas Craig had always in comparison had a somewhat fractious relationship with the York fans. Sinclair was injured in the minibus crash during the 1990 World Cup in Italy that claimed the life of Bournemouth FC's general manager Brian Tiler and left Harry Redknapp severely injured. Redknapp later claimed in his autobiography, *'Arry*, that Sinclair had saved his life by dragging his petrol-soaked body away from the wreckage. The accident, coupled with David Longhurst's death a few months later, caused Sinclair to take stock of what was important to him. He decided to give up his position as chairman and become an Anglican priest.

Douglas Craig bought his shares for a nominal fee. In contrast to Sinclair, his relationship with the fans was characterised by mutual distrust. The mercurial side promoted via the play-offs in 1993, which had so nearly secured back-to-back promotions, was largely sold off by Craig, with cheaper and inferior replacements brought in. Alan Little's side punched above their weight for several seasons, only to be cruelly relegated on fifty points when an improbable set of last-day results dumped us into the relegation zone in the eighty-fifth minute. The following five minutes were the only ones York had spent in the relegation places all season. As the storm clouds gathered and the club slipped back into the bottom division, the fissures in the relationship widened. The fans hurled accusations of stereotypical Scottish stinginess; in return Craig intimated that he had been threatened, intimidated, was wanted dead. So he would walk away. According to him, we now had what we'd wanted all along.

Except the ground.

Before selling up, Craig hived off Bootham Crescent from the club's assets, transferring its ownership to a newly-created company, Bootham Crescent Holdings (BCH). Douglas Craig was one of the BCH directors, along with John Quickfall, Colin Webb and, bewilderingly, the former player who had been voted *York City Millennium Hero* by the fans, Barry Swallow.

In March, Craig sold the now assetless club to John Batchelor, a tragicomic figure almost beyond parody. His long, lank hair framed a pasty face perpetually adorned with smoke-blue glasses. He bore more than a passing resemblance to Timmy Mallett, but unfortunately shared none of his sanity. His background was in touring car racing, where he had been both driver and team owner, changing his name at various times to John Top-Gear and John B&Q to secure sponsorship deals. He had twice stood for parliament, somehow persuading more than 300 people to vote for him each time. Reported – probably by himself - to have paid £4.5 million to acquire York City, in truth he handed over a solitary pound.

Batchelor set about systematically destroying what was left of the club. Schemes swirled round his fevered mind. Schemes which started off as harebrained, then started to turn sinister. He would change the name of the club to York City Soccer Club, to appeal to the lucrative American market. He did. It didn't. He would move us to a purpose-built 15,000-seater stadium. We're still waiting. He would change our crest to incorporate a chequered flag, thus drawing two strands of his threadbare empire together. This ransacking of the club's heritage was also carried out.

Christ, he even spattered black and white squares all over the shirt. Did he also replace the corner flags with chequered flags, or am I inventing things to make him more of a pantomime villain than he was? I think he did, you know. He would buy ITV Digital! He didn't. That even he stayed away was a fair indication that this particular project was surely doomed to failure. He would secure a £400,000 sponsorship – or down payment, depending on your levels of cynicism – from Persimmon Homes. This he definitely did, then promptly squirreled it away in his chequered pockets. The club saw at most a quarter of it. Almost inevitably, York City slipped into administration. Batchelor surveyed the wreckage from his new £250,000 house.

Let's be honest here: Batchelor was not without charm, nor fleeting plausibility. Plenty of York fans bought into his vision to some extent, before the whole thing came crashing down around his deaf ears. A showman and attention-craver to the bitter end, as the club slid towards administration he came out to face the fans in his own inimitable way. Microphone in unsteady hand, he took to the pitch at half-time, to announce his handing of the club over to the newly-formed Supporters' Trust. In the clear-headed morning, he recanted.

He had been at Bootham Crescent but nine months, a gestation period that had nearly resulted in a stillborn club. The Supporters' Trust did take over and we clung on in administration; staved off liquidation. Like a baddie at the end of a horror film that just won't die, Batchelor again tried to gain control of the club by buying it off the administrator. Fortunately, the Supporters' Trust held him off, and for three years the club passed into the ownership of the fans who had fought so hard to keep it alive. Jason McGill took over as chairman in 2006. His job had been made easier by the Trust who, with the help of a Football Foundation loan, had managed in 2003 to acquire a majority stake in BCH, thus securing the interim future of the ground. Douglas Craig will die a rich man.

Batchelor surfaced again a couple of years back as a suitor for Mansfield Town. The small price they would pay for having such a visionary at the helm? He would change the name of the club to Harchester United, the fictional team from Sky TV's Dream Team. Honestly. I'm aware I could put almost anything here and it wouldn't seem out of place – he would sign Billy the Fish to play in goal; half-time entertainment would be provided in the form of naked hermaphrodite cheerleaders; Diana Ross had been bought and would be brought on as specialist penalty-taker – but the truth was that he thought it was acceptable to name a proper football club after that of a niche, defunct TV show. A self-confessed asset stripper of companies both in and away from football, his lunacy shouldn't be used as a smokescreen to obscure the devastation he has left behind in other people's lives as he has bumbled merrily along. Let's allow the man himself to nail his purple Harchester colours firmly to the mast:

'Let's be clear, I want a football club, preferably one in the league. The ONLY reason that I want it is to make money, the only reason that I want to do that is to look after my immediate family. I can only do that by making it work on the pitch and as a result making it work commercially. This would be MY club, if you like what you see come and watch, if you don't, then stay away. I am not even interested in discussing it with "fans", however, I will talk to customers anytime.'

A piece of work, my Gran would have said. And she'd have been right.

At the start of the 2003-2004 campaign, twenty-seven-year-old Chris Brass was installed as player-manager, the youngest Football League manager for more than half a century. Four straight wins in the opening four fixtures got the fans dreaming. Patchier form followed, but a win over Carlisle on 10th January left us just outside the play-off places. For a club which had been and still was teetering on the edge of extinction, it was a more than satisfactory on-pitch state of affairs.

Then we did this: LLDLLLLLDLLDLLLDLLLLD. Twenty games without a win. A run almost impressive in its bleak ineptitude. All those Ls and Ds don't tell the full horror of watching your side sucked almost imperceptibly into the vortex of relegation. Somewhere about halfway through that bald parade of letters, it became depressingly obvious that, despite being well above the safety-zone, we were going to go down. And there was nothing us impotent supporters, nor the inexperienced management, could do about it. That list doesn't tell you that we failed to score more than one goal in any of those matches; that amongst all those defeats were full-blown thumpings from Lincoln City and Kidderminster Harriers; that four of the five draws were 0-0s; that one of those Ls was thanks to a recently-released Jon Parkin coming back to haunt us by scoring two for Macclesfield Town; that the penultimate L was a limp defeat at Doncaster that sealed our fate, and their promotion, in one fell swoop. The Belle Vue full-time whistle that condemned us to oblivion seemed shriller than usual, and lingered longer. Faint snatches of it echo on even now. We'd always been a bit crap, but never non-league crap. There's something dirty and shaming in the loss of League status, and we still haven't washed it off.

A sense of perspective allows us York fans to endure our extended League exile, and to still turn up in decent numbers. Yes, getting thrashed by Canvey Island, having to qualify for the FA Cup or travelling 200 miles to some crumbling village ground where we outnumber the away fans are not things we signed up for when we first started supporting this proud old club. But it's a far healthier situation than the godforsaken alternative of no club to support at all.

As our plane bumped back into Luton, which was still as snow-bound as Poland, I hoped that the current team could continue its excellent run of form to give us a chance of repairing some of the damage caused by Craig and Batchelor. I hoped also that the wintery weather would ease enough to allow a fixture or two before spring. I made my way back from Stoke to York. A long day through Macclesfield and Hyde then back to Hebden Bridge, where the same B&B opened its welcoming doors and closed them behind me against the chill.

It was 16th January, and the fans once again converged on Bootham Crescent well before kick-off to clear the pitch of its frozen blanket. The match against Hayes & Yeading would only be our second of the year, and the first league match since the Boxing Day dismantling of Mansfield. Hayes & Yeading had played two games since AFC Wimbledon had thrashed them 5-0 on Boxing Day, winning both. A 4-2 win over fellow strugglers Ebbsfleet and a revenge New Year's Day win over Wimbledon had left them in thirteenth place in the league, well above where they were expected to be. Martin Foyle had done his usual pre-match trick of talking up the opposition, but in reality this was the sort of match we should be winning if we were to maintain a play-off push. An absolute must-win if we were to keep pushing for an unlikely title.

York started as if they had nothing other than gaining three points in mind. Up front, Brodie and Rankine made intelligent runs for the midfielders to pick out. The team's passing was as crisp as the snow surrounding the pitch. Lawless ran the show from out on the right wing, always running with his head up to pick a pass, always making time for himself on the ball. He prodded and probed for the full ninety minutes, like a particularly tenacious surgeon.

Within the first ten minutes, Rankine, Brodie and Carruthers all had good chances to open the scoring, but a combination of good goalkeeping and poor finishing kept the game scoreless. On twenty minutes, the London side's defence eventually cracked. Meredith's through-ball picked out Brodie, who rounded Overland only to be tripped by his outflung arm. Yet another penalty won by our ruddy-cheeked hero. He was already eyeing up the 'keeper's bottom right hand corner when the referee produced a yellow card to book him for diving. For once, Brodie's palms-up innocence was justified. He had indulged in more simulation than a trainee fighter pilot so far this season, and got away with most of it. This could be chalked up as a cumulative, boy-who-cried-wolf booking for the season to date.

Within minutes, Brodie had made amends, mugging his man on the touchline and firing in a cross for Carruthers to guide home. After another twenty minutes of York dominance, the half-time whistle blew. No further goals had been added; Hayes & Yeading trooped off on the wrong end of a 1-0 first-half thrashing.

York wasted no time doubling the lead in the second half. Carruthers and Brodie switched roles, the former whipping in a free-kick which landed at Brodie's unerring feet via a dodgy Overland punch. Lawless released Brodie soon afterwards, only for last man Cadmore to hack him down on the edge of the area. The inevitable red card ended the contest. Shortly afterwards, the imperious Lawless again fed Brodie, who danced round a kamikaze Overland and chipped in off the post for 3-0. Kevin Gall got a fourth before Hayes & Yeading snaffled a last minute consolation courtesy of another Ingham dash off his line. The 4-1 victory was heartily cheered, as was the news that Oxford had improbably lost at home to Tamworth. Four points off the top. As we shuffled out of the Longhurst, snatches of conversation curled out of the crowd into the winter air.

'They were rubbish weren't they? It could have been eight.'

'Brodie again, eh? We'll be lucky to still have him at the end of the month.'

'...a tilt at the title.'

A couple of months previously, that last snippet would have been met with derision from those around him. On a night when we genuinely could have scored eight, and Oxford had started to show fallibility, the words just hung there, held aloft by others' silent hope.

Cambridge, again. The north-south route to the east of the A1 through Lincolnshire and Cambridgeshire was fast becoming my commute. Another trip to the Abbey, another stay at John's, another night at the Griffin on the way down. Even in the midst of a seemingly random adventure, I was reverting to human type as a creature of habit. I had long dispensed with the map for this part of the country. There are fewer roads to remember than in less sparsely-inhabited areas, and I knew the way from Irnham to Cambridge by heart. I now knew Peterborough's bike tracks better than York's. All this familiarity made things nice and secure, if a little prone to ennui. I resolved to change the route next time I came this way. All this solo cycling was a lonely old pursuit; I would hate to add boredom to the mix.

While I was supping JHB in front of the Griffin's open fire, York's players were playing out a 0-0 FA Trophy draw at runaway Blue Square South leaders Newport County. The subsequent replay was an unwelcome addition to the fixture list. I was sure I was going to pay for my shunning of the FA Trophy, with the inevitable fixture pile-up causing me to fail the challenge. The replay at the Crescent would be next midweek, between the upcoming match at Cambridge and the rearranged league game at Histon, a village which is practically a suburb of Cambridge. A trip home for the Trophy would have meant another out-and-back slog. In my lovely Trophyless world, I could enjoy an extended stay down south off the bike. We won the replay 1-0 with a late Pacquette goal. A few days later, Corby Town were similarly dispatched in the next round, a Ferrell penalty separating the sides. This FA Trophy run was going to cause mayhem if it wasn't stopped. It would be blasphemous to want us to lose, wouldn't it?

Back in the league, York arrived at the Abbey for the first of four consecutive away matches. City lined up with Ben Purkiss at right midfield in place of Lawless, whose creativity and composure were missed throughout the match. Cambridge had the better of the opening exchanges, with Meredith charging down a pair of dangerously-placed free-kicks within the first ten minutes. Shortly afterwards, Parslow raced back to correct his own mistake; having swiped at fresh air to allow the dangerous Robbie Wilmott in, he calmly dispossessed him in the area to avert the danger.

Wilmott, who was a constant menace, soon found himself clean through from a quickly-taken free-kick, but Ingham got down well to save his weakly-struck shot. On twenty-five minutes, York mustered their first attempt worthy of the name. A Rankine flick put in Brodie who dragged his twenty-yard shot just wide of Potter's post. Soon after, Graham's sliced clearance fell to Wilmott, who was denied once again by Ingham. Wilmott added to his collection of missed opportunities by blazing over from the resultant corner.

Cambridge, led by Reason and Carden, were dominant in midfield but toothless in attack. It made for uncomfortable viewing from the away end. As the first half drew mercifully to a close, McGurk put in a fantastic block to deny Crow, and Carden flashed an excellent long-range strike just wide of a beaten Ingham's right post. Brodie collected his ninth booking of the season, which left him one ill-judged dive away from a two-match ban. Wilmott was once more in the thick of it, performing a double pike with twist to convince the ref of the severity of Brodie's foul, before springing back to his blue-clad feet as soon as the yellow was shown.

All memories of the insipid first half were banished within three minutes of the restart. The fantastically-named Rory McAuley conceded a needless throw in, which York took quickly. Rankine collected the ball in the box and used his nous and bulk to hold off defenders, before working the ball to the onrushing Barrett. The midfielder's twenty-yard half-volley flew past Potter with the aid of a slight deflection for a thoroughly undeserved lead. The goal was the catalyst for York to up the tempo. Suddenly, City were first to every ball, the defenders, in particular Meredith, sharper in the tackle. Cambridge were visibly rattled, with several passes going astray to the frustration of the home crowd.

Referee Darren Drysdale, who had played a quirky cameo role throughout, continued his erratic performance by refusing Brodie a free-kick for an obvious foul on the edge of the box. When Brodie was replaced by Pacquette to spare him a second yellow, Drysdale bizarrely decided to chase him off the pitch, like a slow motion Benny Hill sketch.

As the match drew to a close, Cambridge built up some sustained pressure. They forced a succession of corners, clattering headers wide from each one. Goalkeeper Potter even came up for the last one, but it landed in neutral territory. Drysdale belatedly reunited lip and whistle and blew for full-time. An ugly, hard fought win. The ninth in a row in the league. Cambridge must have been wondering what they had to do to beat York this season; three games, three times the better side, for the sum total of one point. York liked it down here. I liked it so much I was going to stay until next month.

At midnight on the 31st, the transfer window's curtains were drawn, with Brodie safely tucked up inside.

FEBRUARY

A mere 3.4 miles separate Histon's Glassworld Stadium from Cambridge United's Abbey Stadium. The journey between the two would be by far the shortest of the whole season. As a result I spent a few days making a nuisance of myself at John's house until the day of the match. John is a resolute non-cyclist: I couldn't even persuade him to pedal the few short miles that day. He drove to the match instead with his uncle, also John, and met up with me and Sam and his colleagues to play some pre-match pool in a pub near the ground. Sando was there as well and now completely resigned to losing the bet. It would take some collapse for us to finish outside the top eight from this position. Although recent history showed that if any team was capable of such capitulation, it was York.

John and I have a bet at the start of each season dependent on whose team finishes higher in their respective league: Huddersfield or York. A football shirt of the loser's choosing is the customary prize. The tradition began in the 2003-2004 season in which York were relegated and Huddersfield promoted from the same division. We've never played in the same league again. I've lost this bet so many times that my polyester debts are beginning to pile up. I owed two outstanding shirts at the last count. I wish that John had made a wager like Sando's. I'd love to spend some time with him wobbling uncertainly round along England's backroads, rather than inevitably owing him another jersey.

In keeping with the welcome offered by several of the smaller teams in the division – Hayes & Yeading and Tamworth for example – Histon, and Graham Eales in particular, had really pushed the boat out to make me feel at home. Graham is a classic non-league club official: club secretary, matchday announcer, programme writer, painter of stands and maker of tea. All roles he takes on unpaid. He had offered us a bundle of free tickets and programmes, and hauled me out on the pitch to be interviewed and to meet a couple of the York players, which resulted in an excruciating exchange with captain Danny Parslow.

'You must be absolutely knackered.' Danny said, grinning and offering his hand.

'Not really, I've not even done five miles since the last match.'

End of conversation. What was I playing at? Why not just agree? Or give a non-committal '*Oh, you know*'? It was ten minutes before kick-off: he didn't want a detailed daily mileage breakdown, he was merely commenting on my cumulative effort in a friendly manner. It's a good job I didn't bring up what I'd been up to a few weeks earlier.

On one of the north-south treks I had found myself near the Buckinghamshire village of Drayton Parslow, where it struck me that if I took an arm's-length shot of the signpost for the village I could block out the extraneous letters with well-placed fingers to spell out D a n Parslow. This sounds simpler than it was. I spent a good ten minutes taking shot after increasingly shaky shot, until I chanced upon the right combination of angle, finger-spacing and jitters to give me the perfect snap. And for what? Who was I going to show it to? *Here Jola, this proves that it was worth all the sacrifice. Dan...Dan...DAN! - I did this for you.*

Danny is a really solid professional and has been a loyal player for the club, but he's not my idol. I'm a bit old for footballing heroes. Yes, it's probably for the best that I kept that one to myself. He made a swift enough exit as it was; I didn't want to spook him into another clinical strike past Ingham.

As recently as 1996, Histon were still playing in the Eastern Counties League Division One, a regional division catering for teams from Norfolk, Suffolk and assorted bits of Essex and Cambridgeshire. The division forms part of the tenth rung of the football ladder, five leagues below the Conference National. Histon were promoted from it at the end of the 1996-1997 season, which sparked a rapid rise. Further promotions in 2000, 2004, 2005 and 2007 brought the little side from the twin villages of Histon and Impington to the Conference National, one step away from the Football League. They started their first season at this level very well, humiliating us 1-4 at Bootham Crescent along the way, and finished just outside the play-offs. The following campaign – 2008-2009 - saw them occupying top spot in November. Alongside the league success, Histon also became the first non-league side to beat Leeds United in the FA Cup, knocking them out in the second round. Their league form faltered, but not by much, and they ended their second ever season at this level in a play-off position. Torquay United eventually squeezed them out over two legs.

This was Histon's third campaign in the top tier of non-league, and it remains to be seen whether the Conference National will be the apex of their considerable achievements or a springboard to even greater things. This time round, Histon were struggling on and off the field and, despite the fact that they remained a tricky prospect at home, we were strong favourites to grab another league win for a frankly ludicrous ten in a row.

I wandered round the perimeter of the pitch to join the 200 or so York fans who were scarcely outnumbered by the home support. Sam delighted in pointing out an advertising hoarding at the far end for a local building contractor: C. D. Hood. I had an instant new nickname and have remained, and I suspect will always remain in Sam's eyes, Seedy Hood.

Brodie was serving a suspension for racking up a lengthy list of yellow cards, so Gash started in his place. Histon started well, forcing a couple of early corners which came to nothing, before bursting through down the right wing where James Meredith might have been expected to be. Ingham raced off his line to cover the mistake, succeeding only in wiping out Tidswell, the Histon striker. The lenient ref gave him a yellow, sparing us the hardship of playing eighty-eight minutes with ten men.

The game settled into a familiar, mediocre pattern. Midway through the first half, York rose above the surrounding dross, putting together a scintillating attack. Gash instigated the move, knocking the ball out wide for a charging Rankine, who rolled it along the edge of the penalty area, where it was struck first time by the onrushing Purkiss. *Purkiss?* What was he doing there? True enough, he was playing further up the field than his customary right back position, but it was still a shock to see him getting on the end of a move. He showed no surprise whatsoever, slamming the ball first time into the bottom corner, right in front of the Seedy Hood hoarding. One nil up and well on the way to our tenth successive win. Things remained the same until just before half-time when Ingham refused to come out for a cross, deciding instead to stay Superglued to his line to allow Hudson-Odoi a simple tap-in for a deserved equaliser.

Nothing happened in the second half. They may as well have not bothered coming back out. The two dropped points were the first surrendered since the Halloween horror show at Crawley. That stretch of games represented two months' worth of consecutive league victories. Sure, at times we'd resorted to anti-football; scoring first and hanging on as grimly as a ledge-jumper having a last-minute change of heart. But if by these means we somehow clambered out of this league, none of that would matter. In any case, nine straight wins was a phenomenal achievement.

This sort of sequence may not cause a ripple on the casual Manchester United fan's placid pool of complacency, but this kind of thing rarely happens to teams like York. We'd won every game for a fifth of a season! It's difficult to be objective, but I genuinely think it must be more fun being a fan of a smaller club. For supporters of the big clubs, all that unbroken success must just get dull after a while. I mean, what's the point? Suffering is good for the soul…in moderation. This run of ours, all the sweeter for its unexpectedness, is a big deal, regardless of what league we're in, whatever the opposition. And by Christ it made the pedalling easier, to be making my way to each match in hope rather than in trepidation.

This kind of York City success appears about as often as Halley's Comet. And us City fans view it very much how people in the Middle Ages would have viewed the astronomical apparition: blinking in awe of its unexpected appearance, deeply suspicious of its presence and worried about what will happen when it's gone.

Four days later, the York players had a chance to set off on another winning run at Kettering Town. I made my way to their doomed Rockingham Road ground, which was under increasingly non-negotiable threat of repossession. Despite playing under the threat of extinction, Kettering were having a successful season. At kick-off they lay only one place behind third-place York. The previous season, we had been hammered 4-2 here, to the great amusement of the newly-promoted side's fans. Their jeering prompted one lady York supporter next to me to call out 'We're all right, we can go home; you've got to live here!'

This season's game was a tough, dour affair, with only sporadic bursts of technicolour football punching through the grey. In the first few minutes, Ingham made a quite astonishing save to deny Poppies' captain Roper the opener, somehow tipping his goal-bound header over the bar from point-blank range. Not long afterwards, Rankine profited from Roper's defensive air shot to hammer in the opening goal from the six-yard line.

All subsequent Kettering attacks were Foyled. Bus parked, hatches battened, bolts drawn. The sizeable, noisy York contingent left Kettering's loveably ramshackle old ground for what would probably be the last time. Regardless of where we ended up next season, if Kettering managed to stumble through this campaign and beyond, they would almost certainly have to find a new ground in which to do the stumbling.

The callous truth is that few, if any, York fans were concentrating on Kettering's plight at the final whistle. Another win meant thirty-one points from thirty-three. Full-time scores started to trickle through on phones and radios. Oxford had been held at home by mid-table Kidderminster. Stevenage, who had been mirroring our upwards charge, had lost at Tamworth. All of a sudden we were a point off the top and in a title race. Perhaps the Histon game had been but a blip on our serene march to the Championship? We had some lowly sides to come, not least Ebbsfleet next up. I can't have been alone in beginning to dream.

Between the Histon and Kettering matches, I'd been to the inaugural JustGiving awards in London. I probably should have pedalled there from Cambridge, but felt no great shame in nipping there and back on the train. This was one extra fixture I couldn't have envisaged. Due to me raising money for the Alzheimer's Society along the way, somebody had nominated me for one of the awards, so Jola and I got dressed up and made our way to town.

Not unsurprisingly, I had no suitable attire in my panniers, so spent an afternoon trawling Fulham charity shops for an outfit. If Jola was ashamed to be on the arm of a man pairing a grey check suit with a tight lemon shirt then she did well to conceal it. The dead man's shoes that had seemed such a good fit in the shop turned out to be a little *too* snug. They cramped my toes to such an extent that I was bleeding and limping by the end of the night. Getting back on the bike would provide blissful relief.

Confident that I wouldn't be called up to collect anything, I kicked the tiny shoes off under the table and listened in admiration to the speakers and winners. The whole audience was moved by the tale of Sophie Atay, a toddler whose parents were raising funds to treat her rare neuroblastoma in the States. One of the awards was won by a couple of guys who had set themselves the goal of blagging their way as far as they could from Manchester, with no money. Dressed in orange prison clothes. Armed with only their passports, they somehow made it to Luanda in Angola.

The evening's key speaker was Major Phil Packer, an incredible man who had suffered a spinal cord injury in February 2008 whilst serving in Iraq. Doctors told him he would never walk again. Two years later, he was preparing to start his second successive London Marathon. Since his injury, he has raised well over a million pounds for a variety of charities. His story was told with great good humour and much self-deprecation. He won a couple of awards, one of which meant a substantial cash prize for his charity, which he immediately pledged to Sophie's parents, urging the members of the audience to follow suit. A truly inspirational man.

That same week, Chester City's long-unpaid players decided that enough was enough, and refused to get on the bus to play against Forest Green Rovers. The Football Conference acted swiftly, suspending them from the league. They were given a miserly week to get their finances in order, which was patently not enough time. A week after the end of the suspension, they were expelled from the league, with all their results expunged. A proud old former League club and its decades of results; its supporters highs and lows; its last-minute winners; its hotly-disputed penalties; its half-time pies and Bovril; its histories personal and collective: gone, just like that.

I had of late, but wherefore I knew not, lost all my mirth. I was nowhere near as despairing as Hamlet, or Withnail for that matter, but the fun had seemed to have gone out of the cycling side of things. The same old routes, limited daylight, dismal weather and postponed matches had led me to forget what the trip was partly about: the sheer pleasure of the open road. The stories told at the awards ceremony and Chester's brutally swift demise had highlighted what should have been abundantly clear – I had nothing to moan about.

Back on the bike the next day, this simple truth was underlined by a perfect day's cycling. Kettering to Ebbsfleet is not known as one of the world's great journeys. It's difficult to imagine Paul Theroux thumbing through provincial train timetables, licking his lips with glee at the thought of getting from obscure Northamptonshire market town to Gravesend suburb. Laurie Lee would perhaps have been less reluctant to spring out of bed one midsummer morning if the destination were industrial, estuary Kent rather than the South of Spain. Your loss, Laurie and Paul.

It felt good to be back in the saddle with some proper miles to attack. We glided together, the Kona and I, through snowy Northamptonshire hills; picking the long way round Milton Keynes rather than surrendering ourselves to the town's plentiful but labyrinthine bike paths. We were aiming for Berkhamsted, home to forumer BifferSpice who had offered to put us up for the night. I should probably stop referring to me and the bike as if we were a couple before I met him. Forumers are by definition supposed to be a bit weird, but bicycle espousal might best be kept under wraps.

We – I, just I - swept through narrow Home Counties lanes flanked by freshly cut, snow-capped hawthorn hedges. The air was thick with their sharp-sweet smell, which was heightened by the crisp winter air. Everything was just right: the bright early morning winter sun glinted off the spokes as they span; there was to be no repeat of the recent snowfalls; a stiff northerly breeze propelled me southwards through villages full of thatched cottages. Wicken, Thornton, Nash; a sequence of villages masquerading as a firm of provincial accountants, was one ten-mile stretch of peerless beauty. Later on, the short road from Wing to Mentmore became one of the most memorable of the whole trip; all Postman Pat dips and sweeping bends. There was nothing that special about it – no mountain pass to negotiate or coast road to hug. It was just a stretch of neatly-parcelled bucolic beauty that could only be English; a microcosm of the country and of the whole ride. Perfection.

From time to time along the way I caught myself singing – Hendrix's *Little Wing* in Wing, *These Things Take Time* by the Smiths in Mentmore. It took a while for me to make the connection that my brain had subconsciously made, then I realised that there's a line towards the end of the song - "*it meant more to me than any living thing on earth*". Too much time on your own on the bike can lead you to believe that such discoveries are much more groundbreaking than they are. Written down, it's plainly nonsense.

People handle long periods of solitude in different ways. My coping mechanism seemed to be to construct and play out an interior monologue as I ground out the miles. Word association with the ever-changing place names; weak and tenuous puns; overblown imaginary *l'esprit d'escalier* reactions to innocuous situations. Sometimes – quite often, actually - I was an erudite, sarcastic footballer giving short shrift to an impertinent post-match interviewer. Kind of like a more insufferable version of Gordon Strachan, if you can imagine such a thing. This was just one persona amongst many in a barely coherent gaggle that roamed freely around my lonely mind. I realised things were getting bad when I named one of them Stephen Pedalus. But I couldn't stop them rising up; for large swathes of the trip I was under attack from the staggeringly banal minutiae of my tiny, fevered brain.

At least today the gaggle's only outward manifestation came in the form of singing out loud. I had chanced upon a glorious route. The day's cycling can usually be graded by how often I stop. Many times indeed on a bad day, but just twice that afternoon. Once was to laugh at a sign outside a nursery which read "DRIVE SLOWLY CHILDREN". Its curious lack of punctuation made me read it as an admonishment to precocious toddlers: "*What have I told you children? No showing off behind the wheel.*" The second stop was for a bite to eat, in view of a railway line where I contentedly watched trains slide into a tunnel, surprisingly expertly for Virgins.

It was the sort of day to make me realise once more how lucky I was to be doing what I was doing. Even the looming spectre of my nemesis the Ridgeway proved easily negotiable. By pure luck, the road I took allowed me to glide smoothly through the only gap in the hills for miles around. I was in Berkhamsted well ahead of schedule, so I treated myself to a pint and waited for BifferSpice to finish work. We'd met before, when some of the guys from the Writers' thread had decided to throw off the cloak of anonymity and meet for a few beers in London. This evening took a similar path, the kind of night where you're enjoying yourself to the extent that you're always one step behind where you ought to be, especially in terms of food.

Biffer took me to one of his locals and thrashed me repeatedly at pool. I had previously thought myself a good player, but his merciless drubbings gave me a harsh sense of perspective. I managed to hold it together enough to beat one of the locals, which was fortunate as I'm pretty sure that he proposed that if I lost I had to perform anal sex on a goat. I don't think he was kidding. His accent was quite strong and he was more than a little drunk. And he didn't have many teeth. But he was thoughtful enough to accompany his slurred speech with some vigorous thrustings against the end of the table. Yes, I think he was genuinely suggesting billy-buggery as a forfeit. I took him seriously enough to focus properly on the game. It wouldn't have been a massive surprise to find out that he had a goat tethered out the back, and you do get some unusual house rules variations. I've never agonised as long over a final black.

After an extended tour of Biffer's favourite haunts, we ended up in a Thai restaurant in an earnest but forlorn attempt at soaking up some booze. Biffer proposed to one of the waitresses, who were resplendent in Harchester purple. She gave him an '*Oh, you!*' look that spoke of previous attempts. She turned him down, again.

A hungover pootle across London brought me to Hither Green and to Adam, who was joining me for the short trip to Ebbsfleet. He'd bought a bike especially and was ready to get in the saddle for the first time in several years for the twenty or so miles through South East London to the industrial Kent coast. Ebbsfleet United used to be called Gravesend & Northfleet, and they still play at G&N's old ground, at the foot of the sharp climb into Gravesend. Ebbsfleet itself is little more than a notional town, the collection of houses and streets around the shiny new Eurostar terminal having been named in advance of its existence.

Before we got anywhere near the proto-ghost town, we had a few ups and downs to negotiate.

I was worried about Adam's brutal reintroduction to cycling. 'Erm, do you know about Shooter's Hill?'

He gave a resigned shrug. 'Yeah, I'll probably have to walk.'

Shooter's Hill is a monstrous incline which seems to rear up out of nowhere. A year ago, Jola had made it most of the way up on her knackered old sit-up-and-beg before she stopped to walk. I had rolled back down the hill to join her, trying to make my relief at being able to dismount look like chivalry. This time round I flew up. Well, at least maintained a dignified and steady pace throughout. It was the starkest representation of how much fitness I'd gained over the course of the challenge. Long, drawn-out hills with a fully loaded bike just simply weren't a problem. I was by no means quick, but neither was I in any danger of stopping to push.

This level of fitness had been hard-earned – cycling between fifty and a hundred miles for twenty days each month had changed my body shape and given me loads more stamina. The gains had been slow, cumulative and incremental: a bit like climbing Shooter's Hill. I was sure that at the end of the season I'd lose the fitness much quicker than I'd gained it, freewheeling all the way down to a town called Sloth.

I waited for Adam at the top. He'd been wrong about having to walk. Once he'd caught his breath we pelted down the other side to Welling and were tucking into a Dartford fry-up in no time at all. A series of tough little climbs left us high above the estuary, where the road ribboned its way past Bluewater shopping centre to the ground.

On my previous visit to Stonebridge Road, I'd managed to grab some time with Will Brooks, with a view to interviewing him. A sometime sports journalist, Will had founded the extraordinary My Football Club in 2008. Tapping into the widely-held belief that us supporters could do better than the manager, if only given half a chance, MYFC pledged to buy a stricken club with the money raised from subscriptions. Those who subscribed would in return be offered a say in decisions on the day-to-day running of a club. For a yearly subscription of just £35, you could make those Fantasy Football or Football Manager dreams come true: through a series of online votes, you could help work out the budget; choose who to sign and who to release; even pick the team.

The question remained: which team? Rumours of involvement with Leeds United and Nottingham Forest were allowed to circulate unchecked. Several clubs in League Two and the Conference were approached, or approached MYFC themselves. Amidst all the speculation, subscriptions continued to pile up. By the time Ebbsfleet was confirmed as the club to be taken over, 32,000 people had paid up for their own slice of chairmanship. Or 27,000, depending on who you believed. Clarity was never paramount for MYFC.

In the months after the takeover, things went incredibly well. Ebbsfleet pulled off an unlikely FA Trophy win which helped to further secure their financial future. The club's thousands of owners voted to sell John Akinde to Bristol City, generating a further £140,000. But many of Brooks' initial promises failed to materialise. MYFC's slogan of '*Own the club, pick the team*' was never fully realised – members never did get the chance to choose the players. Under these opaque conditions, people started to lose interest. When communal decisions were put to vote, fewer and fewer votes were cast. By the time members were belatedly offered the option of whether or not they should have a hand in team selection, only 492 people bothered to vote. The option was turned down. An impassioned plea by manager Liam Daish managed to inspire just enough people to vote against meddling in team affairs.

Will was very accommodating when we met, making time to talk despite his PA having not told him about our appointment. He bought us both a Guinness before the match, making great play of having smuggled me into the home supporters' bar. He was affable, garrulous and good company. Until I asked a couple of more direct questions about the club's financial position and the precipitous drop in subscriptions. One year on, only a small percentage of the original members had renewed their subscriptions, and it was becoming apparent that in this environment the club would struggle to break even. Suddenly he became evasive, less amenable to the mooted interview. I imagine my feeling on meeting Will, of initial exuberance fading to confusion and suspicion, was one with which Ebbsfleet fans could easily empathise. I was really disappointed in how the project had panned out. I remember feeling excited at the idea, toying with joining in. It *had* been a fantastic idea, marred beyond redemption by iffy execution.

By the time Adam and I pitched up at the ground a further year down the line, Brooks and Ebbsfleet were wading through a messy separation. Subscriptions had fallen well below break-even and the club was toiling in the league, its future clouded by financial uncertainty. The thousands who had signed up to the venture in good faith could simply walk away. Not an option for the club's diehards, who were now left facing the unpalatable prospect of steering the club through the choppy wake made by somebody else's flashy speedboat.

Back on the pitch, the most significant moment of the match happened midway through the second half, and nowhere near the ball. Brodie, perhaps frustrated at being marked out of the game by Darius Charles, smashed Dean Pooley in the face with a deliberate elbow. The referee sent him straight off. Clearly embarrassed, Brodie trudged off the pitch with his shirt pulled over his face to cover his reddening cheeks. He would miss the next three matches. And we would miss his goals.

By the time Brodie lost his head, York were already trailing courtesy of Moses Ashikodi's strike just after half-time. In truth we were lucky to have all eleven players on the pitch even then. Five minutes into the game, Rankine clashed heads with Clint Easton, although it looked like Rankine had led with his elbow. Easton was immediately replaced, with what was subsequently confirmed as a fractured cheekbone and eye socket. The referee chose to give Rankine the benefit of the doubt.

It had been a scruffy, disjointed, dirty game, won 1-0 by Ebbsfleet. Both sides would have to be patched up as a result. Despite our lack of injuries, I felt that we would suffer from Brodie's absence more keenly than Ebbsfleet would theirs. Luton were York's next visitors, and they were lurking menacingly one place and a handful of points behind us, with a couple of games in hand. We could do with our brilliant, daft, hot-headed talisman.

As it forms part of the M25, you can't cycle over the Dartford Crossing. Instead you roll up at a hut and ring a bell, then wait half an hour in the thickening drizzle for a man to turn up in a 4X4 to ferry you across. Annoyed that he has been called away from his real work, he sits arms folded behind the wheel as the drizzle turns to heavy rain, occasionally barking incomprehensible instructions. After ten minutes of ineffectual faffing, you manage to tie your bike to the rack, place your panniers on what you couldn't have known was the wrong part of the back seat and hope against hope that your hastily-lashed bike doesn't come loose on the trip over. The man then proceeds to drive in a manner designed to dash your hopes. He asks perfunctory questions to establish what you are doing on a bike, in this weather, you stupid twat.

'York fan, eh? Bunch of thugs.'

'We're not always that rough. I take it you're an Ebbsfleet fan?'

He looked at me as if I'd just shat in my hand and smeared it across his stupid fat face.

'Nah, I'm from the other side, aren't I?' He gestured to the north shore of the estuary, towards where he was driving us. 'I'm a Grays fan, me. Some of the lads at work are Ebbsfleet. Said you was a right set of dirty bastards.'

'I guess Brodie didn't really cover himself in glory.'

'Eeh, t'Brodie din't coover 'imsel' in t'glory?'

'Erm, I guess not.' What was he doing? Had he had a stroke? My accent isn't even that northern. We were halfway across the bridge. If I just kept quiet it would all be over soon.

He deposited me and my kit in a puddle-strewn gravel run-off that led to a busy roundabout.

'Thanks. Maybe see you at Grays in a couple of months.' *Christ I hope not.*

'Doubt it. We'll thrash you anyway.'

Grays thrash anyone? They're absolutely shit! This is what I should have said. Instead I mumbled something about us being sure to give them a good game. *I hope we hammer you. I hope we relegate you. Yes, you personally.*

He had a point lurking somewhere deep behind his complacent gormless chops. We must have looked a pretty dirty team against Ebbsfleet. A deserved red card for one striker's flailing elbow, his strike partner lucky to stay on the pitch after leading with *his* elbow. Objectively speaking, that sounds pretty dirty. But objectivity has never been a football supporter's strong suit. These are *our* lads, fighting for *our* cause, good solid York lads through and through. Until they move somewhere else, the treacherous gits.

I am by nature a late riser, so an uncomfortably early start the next day was a sickening necessity. I only had thirty-six hours to get from Cambridge to York. A fortuitous wind pushed me across the Fenlands' empty, flat backroads. John's latest pack-up had long been demolished by the time I got to Chatteris, which had transformed itself into a mid-morning ghost town. After much fruitless probing, the town eventually gave up a solitary, dust-dry sausage roll. Throughout the day, rain and snow switched roles like co-operative members of a Tour de France breakaway. A lovely route that clung to the side of sunset-tinged canals north of Boston guided me into Market Rasen, where a bedraggled, broken version of something like me checked into a B&B run by the town's mayor. The 108 miles I'd knocked off meant that I'd given myself every chance of making it back to the Crescent in time for kick-off the following night.

I rolled exhaustedly into York in time for a speedy Bay Horse pint with Dad and Steve, getting to the ground just in time for the kick-off of the first of two consecutive home matches, an entertaining enough 0-0 draw with Luton. We followed this up with a lamentable 0-1 defeat to struggling Eastbourne Borough, thanks to a brilliant solo goal from Liam Enver-Marum. Two defeats and no goals in the last three games, and Brodie still had one more match of his suspension to serve. This was more familiar territory for a York fan. Which clown had been talking about a title challenge? I hope they're suitably embarrassed now.

MARCH

Due to the FA Trophy quarter-final at Barrow, I had a few extra days to complete one of the trips I had been most looking forward to. When poring over map and fixture list before the season started, I'd ranked the trip to Forest Green Rovers alongside the one through Dales and Lakes to Barrow as one of the most scenic of the whole nine months. The notional route I drew up took in the Peak District, then went either round or through Birmingham and on into the Cotswolds. Forest Green's New Lawn ground is tucked away in the hamlet of the same name, perched high above the town of Nailsworth near Stroud.

The Gloucestershire club have been punching well above their weight for years, and are one of the longest-serving Conference clubs alongside York. Occasionally reprieved after the season ends due to other teams' financial catastrophes, they have also avoided relegation numerous times of their own accord, finishing as high as eighth in 2007-2008. They were languishing one place off the bottom prior to this season's visit of York, but regardless of where they are in the league when we play them, they usually give us some trouble. Given that we were in full-on collapse mode, most York fans predicted an FGR win.

I used up some of the spare time at my disposal fitting clipless pedals and teetering about the streets surrounding my Dad's flat in cleated boots. I'd had them since the start of the season, so quite why I'd taken this long to fit them I'm not sure. People took great joy in pointing out the steep learning curve in store. You'll fall, they said. I laughed. There didn't seem to be much to it. The key was to twist the foot to unclip at the right moment at lights and junctions. A deft outward flick of the heel did the trick with some aplomb. I found it more difficult to clip back in, frequently weaving dangerously back into traffic as I stamped and fretted at the cleat like a little bull.

Gliding serenely down Hull Road at the start of the 230 or so miles, I was struck by a fundamental, embarrassing truth. Even with all the extra baggage, when clipped in I could pull the pedals up as well as push them down. This may seem blindingly obvious, but the thought had never entered my head before. All that wasted energy in the hills, all that needless toil. Well now I would fly up hill and down dale on my steel Pegasus. Man and machine as one. The match wasn't until Saturday, why was I even bothering to set off on Wednesday? I'd probably be in Stroud for sunset. Waiting at the first set of traffic lights, I realised that I could rest the pannier against the adjacent railings and remain upright. Still cleated, arms folded, I was as smug as any London hipster courier, if a little less nippy.

I made for Tadcaster, mulling over how I felt about York's defeat the night before. Barrow had won 2-1 to end our Trophy run, racing into a two-goal lead before Pacquette pulled one back for a second-string York side to set up a nervy last twenty minutes. Nervy both for the Holker Street faithful and for me. A draw would have been the worst possible result, with a replay adding to an already overcrowded fixture list. The hard winter had left an awful lot of fixtures shoehorned into the last two months of the season. There were still thirteen league games to play, meaning many more miles to add to a total which was already well above 8,000. Any more shuffling around of fixtures or one badly-placed rearranged match could spell the end of the challenge. I had cut it fine at several points throughout the season so far; I didn't want to fail with the finish line in sight.

So how did I feel about the Trophy result? Not exactly happy that we'd lost, but not too put out either. It *was* only the FA Trophy. Probably a bit beneath us, despite the fact that we'd not won anything for years. We were league contenders after all, not some mid-table side content with progress in a minor cup. I'd encountered this type of thinking before: in the midst of all this exercise, I'd morphed into an armchair Liverpool fan.

Sitting stiff-legged on bare concrete, back propped against a cement block in a hill-top lay-by overlooking Wakefield, I had to admit that I was knackered. There must have been something wrong with my go-faster pedals. I'd have to return them when I got back to York. One of the things I'd learnt about touring like this was that you had to be phlegmatic about days when it doesn't go to plan. I'd eaten well and taken on plenty of fluid, sometimes days like this just happened. It was already early afternoon and I was only thirty-odd miles from York. On such occasions, sometimes a second wind kicks in; I might yet make it well into the Peak District; I might not make it to Barnsley. Stroud was a bit of a stretch though.

A few hours and barely a handful of miles later, I was wheezing empty-tanked up a vicious little hill into Hoylandswaine. Stuck in the granny gear with nowhere left to go, I was expending more and more energy to turn the pedals ever slower. I refused to get off and push – partly because of pride, but mainly because no matter how slowly you cycle, it's still better than heaving fifty kilos of bike and baggage uphill. Not too proud to stop and compose myself before pushing on again, I put my foot out to take the weight. There was just enough time before I slammed into the tarmac to remember that I was clipped in, but not enough to do anything about it. The weight in the rear panniers pulled me backwards as much as sideways; the bike and I fell in a quite graceful diagonal arc, like a rocking horse with ballast attached to the rear of one rocker. I landed flat on my back, my right knee pinned by the bike against the road. Some undignified twisting eventually set my foot free of the pedal. Gazing up at the squat tower of Hoylandswaine church, I realised somewhat belatedly that I'd had The Bonk.

This is nowhere near as much fun as it sounds. The Bonk is the term cyclists use for that very specific moment when you're simultaneously overwhelmed by a complete lack of energy and ravenous hunger. When the first wave hits you, it's already too late to do anything about it other than eat as much as you can and wait for it to go away. I'm usually as ill-prepared for The Bonk as I am for everything else, but thanks to the remnants of the packed lunch my Dad had made for me that morning, I was armed to fend it off. Flopping down on the nearest bench to stuff my face, I allowed myself a wry smile: I hadn't bonked in a graveyard since I was sixteen.

Having eventually crested the hill, I took a room in the first pub I came to in Penistone, a picturesque little place full of independent fair trade shops and blessed with views over the Pennines in all directions. It's also on the top of another bloody great hill. I'd unerringly brought myself to the highest place for miles around yet again. Sure enough, a sign proclaimed it to be the highest market town in South Yorkshire. Without Dad's pack-up I would have never made it up there.

I ordered a Guinness, which caused the barman some bemusement. A quick scan showed that everyone else in the pub was drinking lager, but surely he knew how to pour one? To give him some breathing space, I took my bags and, on the locals' advice, my bike, up to my room. When I came back down a full ten minutes later, the barman was still scrutinising the glass, nozzle and pump with wild-eyed bewilderment. It was as if he could comprehend neither the tools to hand nor the intended result, like an illiterate asked to decipher the Rosetta Stone.

To fill in time while his colleague wrestled with my Guinness and his inner demons, the other barman struck up conversation. 'Where have you come from, then?'

I really wanted that pint. I was licking my lips and flexing my fingers like the dark-haired guy who danced around in the old advert, barely able to wait for his Guinness to settle. I waited, but wasn't sure that good things would come.

'York.'

'I went to York once. The beer was crap.' This lacerating snippet of wisdom came from my neighbour at the bar, short and stocky like me but with black hair sculpted with its own grease into a style best described as Playmobil chic. He had beady little eyes and a prominent moustache, both as jet as his hair. He looked like a malevolent Bob Carolgees. His hostile look and opening gambit didn't offer much hope for a conversation, but I had a go regardless.

'There are some really good local ales. York Brewery brew...'

'Crap.' This was clearly his final word on the matter. A wordless jerk of his oily head indicated to his silent wife that it was time to go. He downed the rest of his lager and ushered her out of the door. Everyone else in the bar shouted their goodbyes to him, but nobody spoke to his wife. Perhaps they never did.

'Night, Tony,' shouted the barman.

Well that explained it. The man the whole town was named after: Penis Tone.

I ordered a cider from the other barman to quench my thirst, took it across to a table and sat down just in time to watch the England v Egypt friendly. I returned from a half-time wee to find a poorly-poured pint of Guinness plonked in the middle of the table.

There's an enigmatically-named road in Western Australia called Useless Loop. It came frequently to mind during the first hour of the next day's ride. I set off confidently up onto the moors only to find that the backroad junctions had no signposts, or if they did they bore no relation to the map. An aimless, undulating spin brought me onto a thin strip of tarmac high above a small town. Hoping that it was Stocksbridge, I freewheeled down as far as the welcome sign to Penistone. Just in case malevolent Carolgees had been out in the night switching signs, I checked with a passing dog walker.

'Yes, that's Penistone, like the sign says.' She pointed me in the right direction in the kindly manner of a patient primary school teacher.

Writing the first hour off as the prologue, I raced headlong into the first stage proper of the Tour de Peak District. Well, raced for a mile until confronted by the first of several twenty-five per cent inclines. I spent a beautiful cloudless morning amongst lush green hills and reservoir-studded valleys, chatted with elderly lady cyclists over tea and scones in a hilltop pub, detoured miles out of the way to sweep through Chatsworth's manicured lawns. Had fun, in short.

Late that afternoon, a bright yellow diversion sign was all that stood in the way of a bed in Ashbourne, where I had on a whim decided to stay for the night. When I left Penistone I'd been intending to stay with Dave, an old friend from University who now lives in Birmingham. Even without the prologue, progress had been pretty slow, and the thought of doubling the day's fifty miles was laughably optimistic.

The hills had taken it out of me and it was getting late; there was no way I was going to add even an extra ten miles, so I did what I had done with every other diversion sign I'd come across so far: ignored it. They're for cars really, and even if the way was blocked by barriers or idling machines, there'd be a way to sneak through on a bike. After a few miles of blissful traffic-free road, I noticed a farmer struggling to drag a huge metal gate across the entrance to his field. Just to make sure, I shouted out to him.

'Excuse me, can I get through to Fenny Drayton on this?'

'Fenny Bentley?'

'Er, yes. Sorry. Fenny Bentley.' I must have been thinking of Fen Drayton. I could picture it on the map, between Cambridge and St Ives. I'd spent so much time in the Fenlands that its villages' names had crept into my sub-conscious, and so much time staring at the map that its network of roads and names was tattooed on the back of my eyelids.

'Course you can. You'll get all the way to Ashbourne. Don't worry about that diversion, it's just for cars.'

'Thanks. You need a hand with that gate?'

He looked at me as if I'd just asked him to carry out a Berkhamsted pool forfeit. 'No. I'm fine. Get on, lad.'

Half a hilly hour later, I was stopped short by metal barriers. There was no immediately apparent way of getting through, but there was no way I was going to retrace the last hour's miles. Ashbourne was just the other side of these barriers, maybe two miles at the most. I would rack up twenty-five miles getting there by an alternative route. It was getting dark and I was hungry and tired. I would find a way through.

The barriers were at least eight-foot tall and spanned the whole width of the road. They were kept in place by posts driven into concrete feet on either side. After wiggling one of these feet from side to side for a few minutes, I managed to open up a crack between the post and the verge, just about big enough to get the bike and panniers through in one go. I wasn't about to mess around unclipping and reattaching panniers if I could avoid it. It was tight, but I was soon gliding across the fresh tarmac on the other side, I would be in Ashbourne in no time.

Or would have been, if the road hadn't immediately petered out into a muddy mess. It was like driving from Germany into Poland. The surface had been ripped off, leaving the clay underneath exposed to the afternoon rain. It took me the best part of half an hour to drag myself and the bike through it. The sticky terrain was dotted with broken pallets, deep puddles, discarded wisps of barbed wire and smashed glass. Mud slopped over the top of my boots, reaching half-way up my bare calves. I felt like a WWI soldier carrying a stricken comrade back to safety. The bike sank into the mud up to its disc brakes in sympathy.

More riving of concrete and metal at the other side and we were free. Free to find an accommodating B&B. The owner of the first suitable one didn't seem to mind the dirt, offering me a very kind charity rate for the night, which she didn't rescind even when she brought me up a cup of tea to find me using her kettle to wash the stones and mud out of my boots into her ivory sink.

The next day's cycling was surprisingly easy. In what seemed like no time at all, Birmingham's northern tentacles drew me in, propelled me across the city's vast joyless expanse and spat me out the other side. They spat me out at an unexpected angle, sending me spinning towards Worcester. I compounded the error by heading for Great Malvern. I should have been aiming for Stroud, where I had a place to stay with Andy Ward, a friend of a friend. The knowledge of a bed for the night spurred me on. As did the glorious stretch from Great Malvern to Gloucester - a delightful downhill glide with the Malvern Hills burning red over my right shoulder in the setting sun. By the time I got to Andy's, I'd done 116 miles, more than I'd managed in the previous two days put together.

Andy greeted me like a long-lost friend. Over pasta and a beer we talked about my project, and some of his. He is a sports writer with many assignments on the go, but he was most animated about a collaboration he was working on, an ambitious book tracing the post-war development of British football and its sociological impact on the country. He goes to watch Forest Green quite often, although I wouldn't say I could pin him down as an exclusive supporter of the team. He seemed more of a fan of the game itself; of its foibles; its history; the funny and poignant moments it throws up.

His books are immaculately researched, his shelves stuffed with sheaves of notes, photocopied pages from libraries, ideas for future books. His mind is similarly crammed with an abundance of football anecdotes. We spoke a lot about my trip and Andy always had an apposite tale to tell – a mention of the Alzheimer's Society prompted him to pull out a file full of notes on the link between footballers and Alzheimer's. Talk of Joe Mercer and Jeff Astle segued into obscure anecdotes about Barnsley team coach drivers and York City groundsmen. With only a few miles to pedal to the ground the next day, we spoke long into the night.

In the morning he showed me round town, where a half-hour trip to the farmers' market resulted in meeting the former England Rugby full-back Alastair Hignell, a seventy-year-old footballer and cyclist called Dennis Gould who is one of the Football Poets, and several of my host's mildly eccentric neighbours. Stroud is an interesting, alternative town and I got the feeling that most days would be like this if you lived there.

Having got myself immediately lost trying to find the bike path to Nailsworth, I asked a fellow cyclist if he knew the way.

'Yes. I'm off to Nailsworth myself. Are you Bicycle Kicks?'

'Erm, yes. I guess so. I'm Simon.'

'Rick. Pleased to meet you.'

Rick is a York fan exiled in Bristol who cycles to the Forest Green match every season. It was great to have a bit of company as we pedalled on to the ground, and he kept me entertained with tales of his away days, dating back to City's Second Division mid-1970s heyday. We chatted all the way until the brutal hill just before the ground, where breath was required for other purposes. If only I'd taken on this challenge a couple of years earlier, before they built the New Lawn and moved 400 metres up the hill.

Alongside the usual suspects at the ground I met Matt, a ukulele-playing West Brom fan from Gloucester who'd stumbled across my website when he was thinking about pedalling round after the Baggies for a season. I'd never met the guy before, so it was a bit of a shock to find him cheering me on as I reached the summit. The sparse applause made me feel like a Tour de France rider cresting a *col* long after the rest of the peleton had disappeared down the other side. We pedalled back to Gloucester after the match, where Matt had kindly offered me his spare room, stopping for food and a pint halfway up another hill near Painswick. Rick sent a quick email: he'd made it back to Bristol before we'd even finished our steaks.

Oh, there was a match as well. We lost again, 2-1 this time. Two bouts of comatose defending gifted Forest Green their goals. Ingham watched a cross-shot sail over his head into the top corner for the opener, the entire defence failed to hack clear for Thorne to grab a tap-in winner. In between, Levi Mackin had briefly restored parity with his first goal for the club, a heavily-deflected shot. Three scrappy goals and three points dropped. Three other significant results – wins for Luton, Kettering and Rushden & Diamonds – had dumped us down to sixth place, out of the play-offs. An inconceivable position to find ourselves in after our recent record-breaking run of wins. A season which had been threatening to promise so much was now in danger of falling to bits.

I started to ride back to York for a match with another side from the league's lower reaches, Salisbury City, who would be looking to be the first side to complete the double over us. Gloucester to Birmingham, calling in on Dave this time, Birmingham to Belper in Derbyshire, Belper to York. Two hundred miles in three days. This kind of itinerary was pretty standard fare for most of the trip. The miles had started to stack up – I would pedal well over 1,000 of them in March. It might not seem a lot when spread over the whole month, but the nature of what I was doing meant that it had to be done in fits and starts, with several tight deadlines to meet each month.

The Forest Green match had finished at 5pm on Saturday; the home match against Salisbury would kick off at 7.45pm on the Tuesday night. This left all day Sunday, all day Monday and most of Tuesday to get from Gloucester to York. Not exactly akin to a gruelling Tour de France stage, but then I wasn't riding an unladen carbon road bike either. I was immensely pleased that, eight months into the trip, I was still drawing satisfaction from completing these mini-challenges on time.

All went well on the return journey until a mid-morning stop in Chesterfield on the Tuesday. The innocuous-looking hills around the town had sapped my energy and I began to think I wouldn't get back to York in time for kick-off. I had to sit for a long time on a bench in front of the famous church, my legs as knotted as its crooked spire. I coasted down to the train station and stood a while outside the main entrance.

Would it really be cheating? Thanks to the postponed matches, I had banked several hundred extra miles. What if I spent a few of them now and popped up fresh under York station's broad Victorian arches? I weighed up the pros and cons. Nobody would know, unless I was recognised getting off the train in York. But I'd know, and people had sponsored me in good faith. I *did* have those extra miles in the bank. But I'd promised at the start to laugh off postponements and take them in my stride. How would people I knew react? Jola would think it was pretty funny. Will would be appalled. It would be ninety per cent mock outrage for sure, but he could keep up synthetic indignation for a long time. I wasn't sure I could cope with his Chinese water torture.

Will seemed to be of the opinion that this whole thing was incredibly easy, and that I was a weak man for not making the challenge somehow harder. I was looking forward to our little jaunt to Eastbourne together the following month jolting him out of his complacency. And ultimately that's what swung it. The tortured mental tanglings of a solo distance cyclist made me feel that I had to maintain the moral high ground in order to fully enjoy watching one of my best mates suffer immensely. With weary legs, head and heart I clambered aboard.

The bike, not the train.

Cutting it finer than I ever had before, I made it back to Bootham Crescent just in time to see the players take the field. The Longhurst whispered with pessimistic murmurings. *Wheels coming off... that useless lump Brodie hasn't scored for ages... another defeat today then, Mick?* The nervous chatter of grown men whose carefully constructed promotion dreams were being casually dismantled by indifferent footballing Gods.

The game started as if more than the three points were at stake. Salisbury were fighting hard against relegation, and we obviously needed to do something, anything, to stop the slide. Both teams were nervous; they mis-timed tackles, mis-placed passes, mis-hit shots. On the stroke of half-time, Sangaré punched a Barrett free-kick past Bittner, surreptitiously enough to convince the ref that he'd scored with his head. A scummy way to lead, but exactly the sort of luck we needed to turn the season around.

Not long after half-time, we were treated to one of the best goals seen at the Crescent for many a year. Salisbury's young striker Reece Connolly controlled a cross with his chest just inside the area, then simply slammed a volley over his shoulder into the top corner of Ingham's net without even glancing at the goal. It was the kind of strike that drew appreciative applause from the home supporters - it was the first opposition goal I can remember applauding since 1994, when Marcus Stewart completed a hat-trick for Bristol Rovers by lobbing Dean Kiely from out on the wing near the half-way line.

Not long after Connolly's superb strike, the Wiltshire side added an incisive second on the counter-attack and held out for the win. Oxford also lost, at home to Hayes & Yeading, but we were no longer in a position to capitalise on their misfortune. Stevenage had been the main beneficiaries, with Westley's brand of robo-football grinding out another soulless victory to propel them to top spot. York remained in sixth, a point and a place outside the play-offs.

A couple of days later I was toiling up a narrow road in Marsden near Huddersfield, bound for the rearranged match at Altrincham, hoping to avoid a fifth defeat in a row in league and Trophy. I stopped to read a sign informing me that this ancient route formed part of the old coach road built in 1790 by John Metcalf, otherwise known as Blind Jack of Knaresborough. This astonishing character had been by turns an accomplished fiddler, businessman, soldier, horse rider, and eventually civil engineer despite being blind from an early age as a result of smallpox.

On remounting the bike to recommence my painfully slow climb to the top of the moor, pedalling seemed to be an even trickier proposition than usual. Turning the crank felt and sounded gritty, and it became more and more difficult to simply push the pedals round. Unclipping for fear of falling, I laboured on with the flat side of the pedals. It didn't help. It felt like someone was slowly pouring building sand into the crank and tipping a load into the panniers for good measure. I didn't know exactly what it was, but knew it wasn't good. Rider malfunction could be ruled out as I was well fed and watered. This was a Bike Bonk.

For someone embarking on a trip like this, I was a pretty clueless mechanic. I'd been relying on good fortune and handily-placed welders to sort out anything other than a puncture so far. And I subsequently found out that I'd been performing even this minor operation incorrectly by not setting the inner tubes correctly before inflating. This crass ineptitude undoubtedly added to the number of punctures that led to me getting the train in Sandy on the way to the postponed match against Grays.

Maybe it was the bottom bracket. It sounded like the sort of thing a teeth-sucking bike mechanic might say. I had no idea what a bottom bracket was, but I'd heard it being bandied about by manlier men whose intonation placed it in the same category as blowing a head gasket – a suitably worrying ailment just this side of terminal, and expensive to fix. I know that such a basic lack of knowledge is barely credible for someone attempting a 10,000 mile bike ride, but I'm a huge advocate of winging it, and this rudimentary tactic had been serving me well.

Until now.

The summit arrived just before the pedals seized entirely. Pedalling on the flat was at least possible, so I pushed on. Not that I had much choice; a dark, desolate moor top with no mobile signal offered little in the way of comfort. I decided to freewheel down the other side to Stalybridge, where I hoped the morning would reveal a bike shop capable of drilling out the sand, or whatever was required to allow me to get to Altrincham for 3pm.

Stalybridge did indeed have a bike shop, but it had closed down. I toiled a few miles to Denton, where I stumbled across an open bike shop, but the man didn't have the right part. He confirmed it was the bottom bracket – yes! The tiniest of victories – and loosened it as much as he could. He rang a mate in Stockport, who reckoned he could fix it in time for me to make the match, providing I got there soon. The loosened crank propelled me another half a mile or so before seizing up completely. I had little choice other than to walk the five miles to the shop in the shadow of Stockport's Edgeley Park ground.

My unhappy trudge left the guy no time to do anything other than to take out the bearings, a temporary fix that at least gave me a chance of completing the fifteen miles to Altrincham before kick-off. Whereas previously it had felt like I'd been pushing the bike through hub-high treacle, now I could hardly get any purchase at all. My legs whirred round like Wile E. Coyote's just before he plummets off a cliff. With nothing to hold them in place, the pedals danced a seasick jig in their loose sockets. The resultant bow-legged, lurching motion turned the wheels at little more than walking pace. I got to the ground five minutes before kick-off. The match at least went ahead this time, but a featureless 0-0 draw seemed scant reward for what had turned into an unexpectedly demanding journey.

I stayed with Matilda for a couple of nights, until her local Chorlton bike shop had the time and the parts to fit a new bottom bracket. I was fortunate to have time on my side: the next match at Mansfield was only a day's ride away.

And what a ride it was. What joy to pedal unhindered! Even the countryside seemed to co-operate. Attacked west to east instead of north to south, the Peak District's hills were more easily conquered. I made it to Mansfield four hours before kick-off. Four hours is an awful long time to kill in Mansfield – an inland Barrow with none of its charm. I called Sally, who was coming to the match anyway. She offered to set off from Derby earlier and treat me to dinner. Little sisters can save lives.

In the meantime, I propped the Kona up against a bench in a pleasant little park next to the river Maun, adjacent to Mansfield's Field Mill ground. In fact, it probably used to be the field that led to the long-gone mill. I was fishing around in my panniers for the least smelly bits of non-lycra clothing when an authoritative voice asked an awkward question. Hoping that Doncaster's coppers' beats didn't extend this far south, I looked up from my rummaging.

'Do you mind if I ask you what you're doing, young man?'

'Sorry, I was just getting changed.'

'No, I mean, where are you heading to, what's your journey?'

I pulled on the least disgusting T-shirt, sat down on the bench and trotted out the usual spiel.

'Very good. Do you mind if I sat and chat with you a while?'

'Of course not.' I smiled and waved my hand above the empty part of the bench.

The man plonked himself down and rested his hands on the silver knob of his walking stick. He had the accent, forthrightness and dress sense of Brian Clough. A well-worn flat cap kept the drizzle off his head.

'So you're a writer are you?' He nodded towards my laptop, which I'd left on the bench.

'Well, I'm writing about the trip as I go.'

'Good lad. I'm a writer myself. A poet. Clive Brookes.' He offered his hand. 'Is it funny, what you're writing?'

'Well I ho-'

'I love yew-ma me.'

'Sorry?'

'Yew-ma. Yew-marous tales and whatnot. Here's one for you.' Hands still clasping his cane, and staring straight ahead, he launched into a recital before I had chance to reply.

> *My wife thinks more of the dog*
> *than she ever does of me,*
> *when she's watching the telly*
> *the dog's sat on the settee.*
> *When we have Sunday lunch*
> *the damn dog gets most of the meat,*
> *It doesn't matter when I'm fed*
> *as long as her pet gets to eat.*
> *She grooms, strokes and cuddles it*
> *whilst saying such loving words,*
> *some of the things she says*
> *are expressions I've never heard.*
> *She takes the dog for long walks*
> *and leaves me all on my own.*
> *I wonder if I am the master*
> *or should I be chewing the bone?*

'See, yew-ma? Oh, I love yew-ma.' He chuckled away to himself.
'I'm impressed that you know it off by heart.'
The compliment barely registered. 'Here, have another one.'

> *He stands there bragging, with two black eyes*
> *Through which he can hardly see,*
> *Trying hard to convince his mates*
> *That the other man's got three.*

'But it's not just yew-marous poems I do, no I write about all aspects of life you see. Just whatever happens to inspire me. You know the Byron poem *Apostrophe To The Ocean?*'

'I don't.'

'Well, this is my reply to it.'

Without pausing for breath, he segued straight into his next poem. It was a long one, with no yew-ma to break it up. If Sally hadn't been due to arrive, I had no doubt that Clive could have filled in the time to kick-off by reciting his works for four hours straight. Eventually, he wound up his response to Byron.

'Thanks. He was from round here, Byron, wasn't he?'

'Yes. Newstead Abbey, just up the road. Great inspiration to me is Byron.'

'Are you from Mansfield yourself, then?'

'Originally, yes, but I spent nine years out on the rigs on the wild North Sea. I was a crane operator on the legendary drilling rig *Sea Quest*. I wrote poems in my spare time. The journalists would line up to ask me what I'd written when I came back to shore. The Bard of the North Sea, they used to call me.'

Clive stared wistfully into the distance, as if searching for the shore. I thought he was about to cry or, worse still, recite a lengthy sea poem.

My mobile rang.

'Sorry Clive, I've got to take this.'

It was Sally, waiting at the ground in her car.

I made my excuses to Clive, feeling bad about leaving him mid-reminiscence. He told me not to worry and set off round the water, head held high, gaze fixed on something in the foggy unknown.

After steaks in a nearby pub, Sally and I took our places amongst the few hundred other York fans in the all-seater stand behind the goal. Field Mill has the feel of a proper League ground, with three decent sized stands dwarfing the run-down, condemned-looking one that hugs one of the touchlines. At our level of football this mix-and-match, bran tub approach to stadium architecture is replicated up and down the country. I love grounds like this that have clearly grown organically, with seats, roofs and patchwork stands added as and when the need arose. Give me Field Mill over Oxford's Kassam Stadium any day. I'm dreading the seemingly inevitable day when we're shunted out of Bootham Crescent to a shitty little corrugated heap on a shitty little trading estate on the edge of town.

Home to the Minstermen for more than seventy years, Bootham Crescent is, like many other grounds all over the country, so much more than just a football stadium. Wedged between tightly-packed back-to-back terraced streets just a few hundred yards outside the city walls, it has played host to all those tumultuous cup runs; been a constant background to raised hopes and shattered dreams; groaned under the weight of 28,000 souls; witnessed pure joy and, in the case of David Longhurst, genuine tragedy.

Sure, it's a quirky, crumbling mess, but it's our quirky, crumbling mess. I'd love us to be able to raise the money to patch the old place up, but the former directors' despicable actions and the subsequent tangled financial mess have made this pretty much impossible. In Progress-at-all-costs Top Trumps, pragmatism beats romanticism hands down every time. It's virtually assured that generic houses will soon stand where once stood Bartram, Bottom, Boyer and Barnes, heroes to wave after wave of York supporters. Those names might not mean much to fans of other clubs, but that's kind of the point. My Grandad was in the record crowd of over 28,000 that squeezed in to see the 1938 FA Cup quarter-final against Huddersfield Town. A generation later, my Dad scaled the wall along with hundreds of others to form part of a 13,000 crowd there to see the League Cup win over Leicester City. Bootham Crescent runs in my genes on both sides of the family, as I'm sure it does for thousands of others. I will cry when we play our last match there. And I won't be alone.

If you gave an infinite number of monkeys an infinite supply of cut-price sub-standard building materials, they would come up with our proposed new home *every sodding time*. Leaked mock-up pictures of the purpose-built (why are new stadia always referred to as purpose-built? It's not as if buildings are often thrown up haphazardly around a rectangular patch of grass, on which white lines are daubed as a temporary measure while builders stand around wondering what to do: although aerial photos of Bootham Crescent provide compelling evidence to the contrary) out-of-town 6,000-seater hint at a predictably depressing blend of Meccano and Perspex. One unlikely promotion would mean that we'd be restricted by such a tiny capacity. Like all identikit grounds built over the last couple of decades, it will not inspire affection. Who gets misty-eyed at the Riverside, unless they're downwind of ICI?

Mansfield's Field Mill has more than 150 years of history to draw on: football has been played here since 1861, making it the second-oldest ground in the country after Sheffield club Hallam FC's. Mansfield Town had been running out in front of Football League crowds for as long as we'd been at the Crescent, but a familiar downturn in fortunes had dumped the Stags in amongst the ever-growing band of ex-League clubs trying to scrabble their way back to respectability.

At this stage of the season, they were still in with an outside chance of the play-offs and would climb to within a few points of York with a win. Given our woeful run of form, that had to be the likeliest result. Not so long before, we had been ten points clear of sixth place, now we were in it. The side was sorely missing the midfield creativity of hamstring victim Alex Lawless. We would be lucky to make the play-offs at the end of the season, when but a month before we had been within a point of top spot.

York started the match in strangely confident fashion, with on-loan Courtney Pitt offering real threat cutting in from the wing, when previously all he'd offered us was his surname as rhyming slang. Up front, Gash and Brodie carved out a succession of decent opportunities for each other to waste. In contrast, Mansfield looked like the same bunch of hapless cloggers that had been played off the snow-fringed park on Boxing Day. They offered little threat other than steepling long throws and aimless long balls. The only surprising thing about York's opening goal just after the hour was the manner in which it was scored. Sprinting on to fellow loanee Haswell's through-ball, Pitt stepped inside his man and drove the ball high into the nonplussed Marriott's net from the edge of the area. It was a lovely strike, reminiscent of Brodie's early-season forays from the opposite flank. Having now gone nine games without a goal, Brodie was struggling to get anywhere near his sparkling pre-Christmas form.

Our misfiring talisman was soon presented with the opportunity to end his recent fruitless spell. Pitt, suddenly looking like his youth career at Chelsea and £200,000 move to Portsmouth might not after all have been an elaborate tale concocted by his agent, wriggled through a couple of challenges to win a penalty. Brodie stepped up to strike the ball low and hard to the 'keeper's right, as he had done with every single penalty so far this season. Marriott became the first goalie to guess correctly, springing across his goal to parry the ball round the post. We closed out the remaining half hour as if the recent run of appalling form had never happened. Another 1-0 win to add to the burgeoning collection, the return to form a welcome tonic before the home match with fellow play-off hopefuls AFC Wimbledon. After a couple of days in Derby, I made my way back to York, deliberately heading north-east out of Mansfield to pick up my Uncle Robin's trail on the lovely back roads through Sherwood Forest.

An hour before kick-off, York's sunny skies darkened to unleash a biblical torrent on the city. The downpour was as sudden as it was ferocious. People jostled for meagre cover in shopfronts, the rain bounced hard off slick pavements and the narrow medieval streets flowed like rivers.

The pitch didn't stand a chance. With hardly any warning for the huge Wimbledon contingent, the game was called off. The rain soon abated, but the damage had been done. Huge pools of standing water are not that simple to clear. The away fans made the best of the hand they'd been dealt. The City of York's history, easiness on the eye and abundance of pubs make it a favourite away trip for many fans, whatever level of football its team is playing at. Wimbledon had brought about a thousand supporters, many of whom nevertheless carried out their plans to make a weekend of it up north. Few would be likely to come back for a likely midweek rearrangement. Quite where the rearranged game would fit into an already shambolic-looking end of season fixture list was anybody's guess. I felt the deadlines tighten around me, but had little option other than to push on to the next scheduled match at Kidderminster Harriers.

Undeterred by my previous visit, I decided to make once more for the Peak District. In truth I had little option, given that Kidderminster lies to the west of Birmingham and the most direct route from York cuts straight through the National Park. Darkness fell as I crossed Sheffield, a city I hardly know despite having lived near it for more than half my life. I was taken aback by its sprawl, pleasantly surprised by its trams, amused by its puny cathedral and intimidated by the hills looming in the dusk along its southern edge. I stopped for the night near Baslow after an hour's eerie pedalling in the deathly, misty still.

The following day's trip to Stafford was punctuated by unnecessary detours along empty roads, stunning scenery and a well-timed bike path. An hour after packing up the tent and still shaking the sleep from my brain, I was surprised to be due west of Baslow. I should have been travelling south or south-west. I was already tired and hungry and found myself attacking a steep incline up to Monsal Head, a breathtaking limestone ridge that keeps watch over Monsal Dale. Well, attacking is too strong a word: it suggests some level of intent. I was sweating, whimpering and pleading with the hill to go away. It wouldn't. Too knackered to even contemplate unclipping, I keeled over into the verge, which was sufficiently banked to allow me to pretend to passers-by that I was simply admiring the magnificent view at a jaunty angle. Their stifled sniggers really spoiled the serenity.

Shortly afterwards, I stumbled across the Monsal Trail bike path. It runs along the old Midland Railway route, following the course of the River Wye and the beautiful valley that it has carved through surrounding limestone peaks. Another hour's blissfully flat cycling brought me out near Bakewell, a handful of miles south of Baslow, with half the day gone. I pointed the Kona south-west and made for Stafford. It was a tiring, confusing day; somewhere along the way I winked at a magpie. Not accompanied by a superstitious wave or anything, just a salacious wink at an unsuspecting bird. I rolled into Stafford – three-time Drabbest County Town winner - with an audible sigh of relief. A gentle arc round Wolverhampton and a dawdle along a canal path brought me into the heart of Kidderminster, and back to Helen and Gary's.

Dave had made his way over from Birmingham to take his place as an Everton-supporting neutral in the away end. We left Gary, a Harriers fan, at the gate and half-heartedly wished each other a good game. As Dave and I joined most of the thin smattering of away fans in demolishing one of Kidderminster's award-winning pies, the Aggborough tannoy man played the Emmerdale theme tune to welcome our players on to the pitch. A decent joke, but it was about all the home fans had to laugh at. A tight game reminiscent of the win at Kettering ended with the same result; Neil Barrett's close-range hooked volley securing all three points for the marauding Minstermen. Just as at Kettering, results elsewhere had gone our way. Wimbledon's defeat and a draw for Mansfield put us firmly back in pole position for the play-offs.

A couple of days later, I was back in York for the home match with Tamworth. It was another nothing game, mere punctuation in the story of the season. Centre back Luke Graham grabbed his first goal for York with a header just after half-time. We seemed all set for another 1-0 win when Chris Smith did something he never managed to do in his three-season spell at York: score. His one-yard tap-in levelled the scores just before full-time. I pedalled straight off after the match; I had just over three days to get to Grays. Again.

I had already clocked up well over 1,000 miles in March before the long haul to Essex, which turned out to be a painful slog into wind and rain. Somewhere south of Scunthorpe, I slumped exhausted against the Trent's retaining wall. Peering into my handlebar bag, I glimpsed a long-forgotten Soreen loaf glinting in the shadows, its wrapper making the bag glow like the suitcase in Pulp Fiction. I wolfed it all down, probably providing me with enough calories to make it all the way to Grays. Its chewiness gave my jaw such a workout that I could barely speak for a couple of days. This hardly mattered, as I didn't really meet anyone to talk to. It was a filthy horrible trip.

But what was that, spearing through the gloom in all its ill-conceived, concrete glory? Basildon! Behold its dreadful Plaza! Get hopelessly lost in its samey streets! Marvel at the sheer audacity of its Hollywood sign rip-off! Tinseltown and New Town, together at last.

I was staying with my friend Haydn, who'd moved here to work at the hospital. Over a beer, he confirmed that the town was indeed as grim as it looked, but that in life sometimes difficult patches have to be endured, in the hope that some good will eventually come of them. As a Luton fan, he was speaking from a position of some authority. We traded pessimistic views on how our respective seasons would pan out, and drove down to Grays. I had already covered the few extra miles to the ground that day before turning back on myself to return to Haydn's, so in effect was already on my way back to the home match against Altrincham. I was happy to be in the car after a long day – seventy-two tough miles into the wind had caused a few wobbles on the way. But I had refused to look back in Ongar, forcing myself to eke out the last few of the 240 miles since Saturday's final whistle.

The game was a strange, listless affair. Grays Athletic was another club under serious threat of closure. Most of the first-team players had long been shipped out and replaced by youth-teamers, who were gaining valuable experience of being roundly thrashed each week. With relegation already guaranteed, the locals were turning out in even less force than usual. I'd watched the corresponding fixture last season – an abject end-of-season 1-0 defeat (featuring Simon Rusk's cowardly stamp), that had many fearing we'd be relegated to the Conference North – from the press box which was directly opposite a low-slung stand overlooked by apartments whose balconies afforded a great view of the action.

Bill Shankly once said 'If Everton were playing down the bottom of my garden, I'd draw the curtains.' Glancing up from my notes, I saw a man pull down his blinds to live out Shankly's cliché. It had been an awful match last year, but with this level of local support in what had been a relatively successful season, it wasn't hard to see that Grays would eventually run into financial difficulties.

A year on, the men-against-boys training match was played out in front of a tiny midweek crowd. There were maybe a hundred of us, and two hundred of them. You could hear the ball thwack against shin pad; make out the players' cries. In this subdued atmosphere, York strolled around the park, stroking the ball about at will.

Grays' young lads were game, but not good or strong or fit enough to hold out all match. Harsley opened the scoring after half an hour with a deft finish. Brodie added another two before half-time to end his drought. Barrett completed the scoring soon after the break and the match meandered to a close. Some poor soul was going to have a terrifying trip across the Dartford Crossing the next day. It had been as downbeat a 4-0 victory as you can imagine. York had to remain professional enough to focus on the job, especially when all the other teams around us were beating Grays with ease. We still had to play them at home, where another ruthless display would nudge us closer to securing a play-off place.

I slept well that night in a real bed. I had nothing left in my legs; the wind had broken me. Nevertheless, I was looking forward to April's six matches and some companionship in the form of trips with Will and Sando. The season proper was scheduled to finish at the end of April with a trek to Stevenage, who had now opened up some clear space between them and Oxford at the top of the table. A few more snaffled victories for York would open up the very real possibility that the season, and the quest, would tip over into a bonus month.

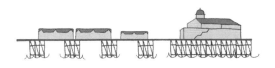

APRIL

'Is that? It can't be.' Sam sped ahead to inspect the sign. 'It is. Norfolk, bloody hell!'

It was as well. Confirmation, in big bold capitals: **NORFOLK** and underneath, Nelson's County. Horatio would never have strayed this far off course, even with one eye. Nor would Lord Hood, for that matter, but his navigator's instinct had been diluted by the generations to the extent that his descendant stood perplexed in a Cambridgeshire fen. Sam got back on his bike and crossed the border.

I called after him. 'I'm sorry mate, I feel like I've misled you. I mean, well, I obviously have misled you. We shouldn't be in Norfolk.' Nelson would have phrased this better - he could hardly have phrased it worse - after all, he had once said 'I cannot command winds and weather'.

Which was as good an excuse as any. After a night at John's in Cambridge, I had cycled the few miles to Earith, where Sam and I had agreed to meet. As he unpacked his new bike from his car in the riverside car park, we were blasted near-horizontal by the wind whipping off the Great Ouse. That same wind ushered us through Chatteris, urged us on past March and deposited us in Norfolk. It was a brutal south-westerly as strong as any wind I'd encountered so far. We had little choice other than to head north-east on a road that ran parallel to one of the arrow-straight diversion channels that criss-cross the fens. Neither of us spoke of the elephant in the room: Sam had to cycle back into this.

'You know what, Seedy Hood? I think it's time for a pint.'

The Globe Inn in Upwell obliged. Landlord Duncan offered us a selection of local ales and no choice at all when it came to food. He did cheese and pickle toasties, nothing else. He told us he was a fan of King's Lynn FC, wound up a few months previously for the want of £77,000. It's difficult to swallow talk of the game's rude health when clubs can go to the wall for a sum smaller than many players' weekly wage. A new club, Lynn FC - quickly renamed to King's Lynn Town FC - had already been formed and would compete the following season.

As we supped, he span tall tales of travellers who'd stopped at his inn. Of Dutch policemen who'd ridden to Upwell from Holland on penny farthings; minor celebrities Sam and I had never heard of; a rich Italian couple whose hotel had been double-booked, causing them to stay in the pub's caravan.

'That one out the back?' Sam asked, for both of us. We'd noticed it as we were locking up the bikes, filthy and half-hidden amongst a pile of rubble and wood.

Duncan caught our incredulous looks. 'I think they were used to more home comforts.'

Three pints and three toasties later we went our separate ways. Sam offered his head to the teeth of the gale whilst I tried to steer myself northwards. Somewhere north of Wisbech, I got lost in a web of signless farmland backroads, so I tried to navigate by keeping the wind at my back. I had no idea where it was pushing me, but I was sure it would all come out in The Wash.

Having eventually found a sign-posted road, I followed it to Boston and stopped for a rest on a bench. The whistler was nowhere to be seen. I checked my phone and found a text from Sam: *Keith Walwyn's just crossed the road in front of me.*

Walwyn is Sam's all-time favourite York player. Born in the West Indies, the six-foot striker became a cult hero at Bootham Crescent for his all-action style and goal-scoring prowess. He ended his lengthy spell at the club as its second all-time top scorer. Pedalling into the wind was obviously torturing Sam's mind: Keith had tragically died in 2003 following a long-term heart problem.

After I'd put up my tent in an out-of-season municipal campsite in Woodhall Spa, I gave Sam a ring. The ride back into the wind had left him a husk of a man, but he managed to communicate by a series of grunts and wheezes that his girlfriend Gemma had provided him with beer, food and a hot bath. Sando and I were supposed to be staying with Sam the night before the Stevenage match at the end of the month, with Sam joining us for the last leg. Hopefully the wind would be kinder for him. It couldn't be any more savage; I was propelled a hundred sleety miles home the next day.

A week or so later, four men in their mid-thirties, both in years and in waist size, were sharing a table in the beer garden of the Exhibition on Bootham. They probably wouldn't have known each other, and certainly wouldn't have all been here at the same time, if it weren't for York City Football Club.

Actually, three of us would have known each other: Will, Matt and I went to the same school. Matt and I started Fulford School together at the age of eleven. We have played a lot of mutually inept playground football, and have witnessed a lot of only slightly less inept York City performances together. Will joined our school when he was fourteen, sweeping into a science class mid-lesson and bravely announcing that he was a Littlehampton Town fan. Even more bravely, he voluntarily offered up their nickname: The Marigolds. Will soon adopted his new home-town team and we travelled all over the country watching the excellent mid-1990s side. This week, we were travelling all over the country to watch them again, but this was the first time by bike. Matt had watched many of those heady 1990s matches too but rarely with us because, well, him and Will couldn't stand each other. Whatever teenage rage propelled their hatred has long since petered out; they clinked glasses to the impending victory which would secure our play-off place.

The fourth man, Sam, returned from the bar with a round, which he placed on the table in front of him, along with a packet of Fruit Gums.

'Can I have one?' I asked, presumptuously picking up the packet from in front of Sam, who whipped it out of my hand.

'No. Not yet.'

'Why not?'

Sam glanced around the table. He had only just met Matt. Will would be staying at Sam's house in Huntingdon that night, but they had only known each other for three hours. Sam knew me better than he knew the others, but in total we had only spent a couple of evenings and one wind-blighted day in each other's company. We could see him weighing up whether or not he should tell mere acquaintances something intimate, calculating the risks, before deciding to go all-in.

'Because I can't open the packet until after kick-off. It's something I used to do as a kid. Just a childhood ritual, but I've dragged it with me into adult life, like a confectionery security blanket.'

He stopped himself and looked up, suddenly fearful that he'd left himself wide open to mockery. But we didn't mock. It was obvious in the shy way he had introduced the subject that it was something important to him. Spurred on by the lack of derision, he let us in on the secret of his Fruit Gum superstition.

Sam first started to watch City at the age of seven. Sometimes just with his Dad, sometimes with his mate Dan and *his* Dad, whose nicotine addiction was responsible for innumerable York goals. There is no scientific proof or documentary evidence of this phenomenon, but apparently whenever Dan's Dad sparked up a cigarette, a City goal would invariably follow. Sam must have been influenced by this terrace superstition, because soon the packet of Fruit Gums which he brought to every match began to predict the future.

Sam was lucky enough to have an endless free supply of the chewy sweets. His Gran worked at Rowntree's chocolate factory and had the right to buy slight seconds at a huge discount. My Gran and Grandad both worked all their lives for Rowntree's cross-town rival, Terry's, and were afforded similar privileges. Long after she had retired, we would frequently go with Gran to raid the seconds shop. Sensibly, kids weren't allowed in, so we would wait in the shadow of the factory's handsome clock tower for her to re-emerge clutching bags full of dented Chocolate Oranges and boxes of not-quite-All Gold. Living on opposite sides of town, and unbeknownst to each other, Sam and I shared golden tickets to Willy Wonka's factory.

The two philanthropic chocolate giants, whose workforces once populated a big chunk of the Bootham Crescent terraces, are now virtually unrecognisable. Rowntree's was bought out by Nestlé in 1988. Nestlé delighted away supporters and shamed the home fans when they bought naming rights for the stadium, renaming it – I can barely bring myself to type this – Kit Kat Crescent. An agreement from which we have now happily had a break. Terry's was subsumed by Kraft, which now makes Chocolate Oranges under licence in Poland. When I was ringing round for sponsorship for the trip, I had called Kraft's marketing department. I explained what I planned to do and mentioned that my grandparents had toiled all their lives for Terry's. The woman on the other end couldn't have been any less interested, and didn't even try to mask her disdain. I may as well have been talking to a Chocolate Orange.

The beautiful old Terry's factory now looks out over the wide expanses of York Racecourse with blank eyes. It closed its doors for the last time in 2005. It will undoubtedly soon be renovated in a bid to quench York's unslakeable thirst for empty buy-to-let flats.

Quite how Sam's Fruit Gum prediction system evolved is unclear; its origins are lost in the mists of time. What is certain is that a young Sam would hold the hallowed tube in trembling fingers until the referee blew for kick-off. Upon the first peep of the whistle, its virgin foil would be broken and its prophecies revealed. The colour of the first Fruit Gum out of the packet would determine the result of the match. Yellow meant a certain York win, black a certain defeat. The darker the colour, the worse the outcome. Green and orange also pointed to home wins, red at best a draw.

'Your system seems to be weighted heavily in our favour,' said Matt.

'Well, I'm an eternal optimist.'

'But it can't just be mindless optimism if it's backed up with results,' I said.

Will hauled his logic into the debate. 'I reckon the system evolved to suit the team and its performances. You only went to home matches as a kid?'

'Yes.'

'Well home sides – even York – win the majority of their matches. And the team you started watching *was* the all-conquering one managed by Denis Smith.'

'All right mate, don't piss on his childhood dreams.' I loved this sort of stuff, and wanted it to be true. 'Anyway, we'll get to see the oracle in action soon. You say it's never failed?'

'Never.'

We arrived at the Crescent just in time to join in the minute's applause for Syd Storey, a member of the remarkable Happy Wanderers side who had recently passed away. Storey played for York for nine years before moving on to Barnsley, and played right up to the age of forty. He worked down the mines from the age of sixteen, work he kept up part-time throughout his football career. He was by all accounts an immensely likeable character, respected by team-mates and fans alike. *A Kestrel for a Knave* writer Barry Hines liked him so much that he named a character Sid Storey in his play *The Price of Coal*. Would that we had the likes of Syd and his mates in today's team to haul us out of this non-league purgatory.

We won the toss and chose to attack the Longhurst end, which rang with predictable boos. The home faithful never like to see their side attack the far goal in the second half, preferring matches to conclude right in front of them. This never used to be an issue years ago; the supporters simply changed ends at half-time using the tunnel which ran under the Pop Stand. Syd Storey would have always attacked towards his own fans. I suppose that people were rarely sliced open with a flat cap and a rattle, but it's a crying shame that we can no longer be trusted to walk past each other in peace at half-time. The tunnel remains, but that particular freedom no longer does.

As the players crossed over in the centre circle, I glanced down at Sam who was standing in front of me. He span the omniscient tube solemnly in his palm to mark the change of ends.

We attacked from the off. Rankine, recalled to the starting line-up, immediately lolloped through the middle and latched onto a Barrett through ball, brushing off the Dons' centre back and captain Paul Lorraine in the process. He burst into the box and shot across James Pullen from a narrow angle. Sam broke the foil just before he shot. The ball nestled in the corner of the net. Yellow. With another yellow underneath for good measure.

'At least a two nil win,' beamed Sam.

Wimbledon, despite barely having eleven fit players, being up against a vociferous home crowd, an early goal and clairvoyant sweets, attacked throughout the match. It was probably their downfall. We broke incessantly, with Barrett and Lawless Lawless carving them open at will. A goal kick from Ingham was flicked on by Rankine to Brodie, who collapsed in the box for his umpteenth penalty of the season. He converted it with precision, low and hard to the 'keeper's right, clattering it in off the post. Another Barrett through-ball released Brodie again, who skipped surprisingly daintily around Pullen and rolled the ball into the unguarded net.

Shortly afterwards, Brodie was once more felled in the box. Some of the many penalties he's won this season have been iffy, some of them outright dives. This one was neither. Brodie was almost on the goal line, meandering away from the goal, posing no threat whatsoever when Lorraine simply steamed studs up into him at calf-height. Brodie didn't have chance to dive this time: he didn't even see the tackle coming. He picked himself up and found the same corner of the net for his third hat-trick, and thirty-third goal of a barnstorming season. Four goals in thirty-five minutes; all scored in front of the City faithful, whose boos of consternation had been replaced by delighted, play-off bound cheers. Lorraine had been run ragged to the extent that he didn't come back out after the break.

He didn't miss much. The second half was understandably anti-climactic. To their great credit, injury-hit Wimbledon, who had only named four substitutes, continued to press forward, but their small knot of fans was destined to head home without even a consolation goal to celebrate. They had arrived in great numbers for the original postponed match, but those numbers were understandably greatly reduced for the midweek rearrangement.

Midway through the second half, Sam uncovered the last Fruit Gum. It was black. Ingham's decision to change ends had saved us from certain defeat. Whilst we were coming to terms with this revelation, Rankine added a fifth from close range. I couldn't tell you much about it though, having not been allowed to change ends at half-time. The Shipton Street Sages wondered aloud why we didn't play like this every week, conveniently forgetting that if we attacked in such a gung-ho fashion against less obliging, less depleted sides the team would be beaten, then roundly booed. By them.

At least Ingham had one less detractor for the rest of the campaign: my Dad had gone to his house in France for the summer. Having watched so many matches together this season, I felt strangely bereft not to be able to hear his unique blend of needless goalie-taunting and after-timing wisdom.

We were back in Huntingdon less than three hours after the final whistle, Sam's car making short work of the miles that Will and I had taken two days to pedal. When we arrived at his flat, Sam poured himself a well-earned beer and sat down to watch a grainy Keith Houchen knock Arsenal out of the FA Cup yet again. He tried once more in vain to pick himself out in the heaving mass behind the goal, and pointed out the surge caused by a near-miss which knocked his sacred Fruit Gums out of his hand. City hadn't needed them that day. At half time we turned to Will, who had never seen the footage before, for some expert analysis. Even Alan Hansen in his most disinterested, laconic state would have offered up snappier soundbites. For the second night in a row, Will was curled up fast asleep on a sofa.

In his defence, it was midnight on Wednesday. We had only set off from Bootham Crescent, 150 miles to the north, two-and-a-half days before. The rearranged Wimbledon match had left us with two-and-a-half days to pedal the 300 miles from York to Eastbourne. Will wouldn't make it; I wasn't sure that I would. So we got creative. We set off on the Saturday, straight after a last-minute Brodie penalty had secured us a 2-1 home win over Altrincham, with the aim of getting to Sam's for Wednesday afternoon. He would drive us back up to York for the match, then back down to Huntingdon, where we would pick up the Eastbourne trail again.

'So you don't think we're cheating?' I asked Will as we bowled along Dr Beeching's dead straight bike track between York and Selby after the Altrincham match.

'Of course not. You'd pedalled up to York weeks ago for the Wimbledon match. It's not your fault that it was postponed. We've got two home matches in three days; we're just getting a head start. York to Eastbourne in two days is impossible.'

This from the man who had practically disowned me for having the temerity not to cycle from York to Oxford prior to the first match of the season. I had decided, before the fixture list came out, to start the challenge at whatever stadium we kicked the season off at. Will was adamant that I had to start in York, even if the first game was on the south coast. I wisely decided to ignore him; it was my challenge, so I could set my own whimsical rules. In any case, I don't always listen to Will. We haven't been friends for this long, and certainly wouldn't remain so at the end of this trip, if we didn't ignore each other's inane ramblings from time to time.

'I can't help thinking you'd be adopting a more sadistic stance if you weren't coming with me.'

'Well I am, so I'm not. Come on, I can't wait to get to Selby. I'm starving.'

I was pleased with Will's about-face, but still couldn't quite believe what he was saying: nobody ever looks forward to going to Selby.

For several years, Will and I spent every other weekend together there. We played for Selby RUFC throughout our teenage years. Will was an enthusiastic, injury-prone second row and I was a competent, tackle-shy scrum half. During one match, loitering well away from potential danger on the other side of the pitch, I clearly heard Will's collar bone crack as he made a tackle. This was the worst of the many injuries he picked up at Selby, but his sporting mishaps weren't solely confined to the rugby pitch. He had once arrived at school with the left side of his face three times bigger than the right. Will is a pretty good cricketer, but a misjudgement in the nets had caused his graceful cover drive to crash into his eye socket instead of the imagined boundary rope. His gymnastic pitch invasion at Hayes & Yeading was merely the latest in a long line of farcical injuries. I wondered what misfortune awaited us on this trip.

We left Selby this time without incident. Pausing only for a sportsman's McDonald's, we picked our way south across the lovely farmland backroads towards Snaith. As a misty dusk descended around us, we settled into what would become a familiar rhythm. Will's much longer legs seemed to allow him to pedal less frequently than me, whilst my little ones had to whir round much more quickly to keep up. I'm sure this can't be correct, it must break at least one law of physics, but it certainly seemed to be that way. We were the quintessential big-man-little-man combination: Niall Quinn and Kevin Phillips out for an evening spin. We pedalled two abreast in companionable silence, knowing without needing to mention it that we'd be stopping in Snaith for a pint.

'Si?'

'Yes, mate?'

'This is the furthest I've cycled in twenty years.'

We were sitting at the bar in the Black Lion in Snaith, all of twenty-odd miles from York. Will had just treated the locals to a graceless dismount from his steed, landing a Lee Champanesque chin in the gravel in full view of the picture window which looked out over the beer garden.

'Well we've already knocked off an impressive twenty miles, mate. Only 300 to go. You still think we'll make it in time?'

Will took a long, contemplative pull of his second pint of Old Peculier. 'I'm sure we will.'

We decided that we would make a few more miles and fling the tents up on the banks of the canal near Thorne. We left the Black Lion, as one always does, with reluctance. I had stayed there earlier on in the trip, and the landlords had made a kind donation to the Alzheimer's Society. This time round, without exception and without being prompted, all the locals dug deep in their pockets to donate. Perhaps they thought we were part of a travelling troupe, and Will the jester.

A mile or so out of Snaith, our romantic waterside camping plan lay in tatters. As we crossed a bridge over one of the region's many canals, there was an almighty screeching of tyres behind us, followed by a dull thud. Hardly daring to find out, I peered over my shoulder to make sure Will was still behind me. Thankfully he was, so we pedalled on round the corner, stopping as soon as it was safe to do so. I went back to find out what had happened.

It was incredibly dark and I could see nothing at first, but on closer inspection found a curved slick of rubber, which became a curved strip of mud and grass. At the end of this rutted rainbow sat a Renault Clio with its nose buried deep in the retaining wall of the bridge. The occupants got out: a woman and her son. The woman took a moment to compose herself before launching a tirade of impressively foul abuse at me. She agreed that we were well lit up and highly visible and not responsible for the accident. Her main gripe being that I had taken so long to come back and make sure they were OK. I tried to explain that I'd come back immediately but to no avail. They had obviously rounded the corner and crested the brow too quickly and seen us at the last minute. A combination of shock and embarrassment had stripped her of all reason.

Will arrived on the scene and, despite their protestations, we called the police. An unmarked car arrived shortly afterwards and drove straight past the whole spectacle, its driver choosing instead to attend to the burglar alarm which had been set off in panic in the neighbouring house. By the time he'd finished, the woman had reversed the Clio out of the wall, made us take note of her number plate, apologised for her prolonged and innovative bout of swearing, and buggered off home.

'Evening lads, not seen an accident have you?'

'Yes, we reported it ages ago. You drove straight past it. They've gone home.' It was gone 10.30pm; Will was in no mood for niceties. Slightly shaken by the near miss, we ditched our plans of camping wild and found a B&B in Thorne.

'Lincolnshire's crap.'

Will sat next to his bike at the bottom of a smallish hill, a sharp rolling down-and-up much smaller than the Ridgeway he'd just manfully conquered. He had managed the long, slow grind to the top with impressive ease, only to be undone by this relative tiddler a few miles further on. All the momentum he'd gained from the downhill stretch had been lost as the hill rose sharply from its base. He sort of rolled backwards and forwards for a bit before settling into the hollow, like a Newton's cradle coming to rest.

'It's not though, is it?'

'No. It's lovely. But not with this wind. And this is by far the furthest I've ever cycled. I'm fucked. I can't cope with this, mate.'

We had spent the whole day since leaving Thorne riding straight into the teeth of a brutal wind as bad as any I had encountered so far; the soul-crushing bone-chilling blast into which I battled through the Fenlands a few months before was no worse than this. The one that had done for Sam a week before might have been worse, but I had always had it at my back. We had covered about seventy miles and still had fifteen or so to go. Will had been pedalling for eleven hours, had been shat on by a pigeon, had taken with exceptional good grace my unerring ability to navigate us to the highest point for miles around, had cycled fifty miles further than he ever had in one day before and had been incorrectly told several times that only three more hills separated us from the mythical, welcoming Griffin at Irnham. He had quite frankly and quite rightly had enough.

I still hated the wind, of course, and always will, but it's a mark of how much fitter I had become that I didn't really feel the hills any more. Eight short months earlier, I would have been sitting weeping beside Will at the bottom of this hill, bike similarly cast aside. As it was, it fell to me to coax him back onto his bike and over the remaining hills with promises of good beer, great food, a roaring fire, a steaming hot bath and a welcoming bed. It was a tough job; he was like an inverse Tommy Simpson. He was never in any danger of shouting out *Put me back on my bike*.

Chris and Liz, as always, didn't let me down. Within ten minutes of our eventual arrival we were sitting in front of the open fire with a wonderful pint of JHB, the steeds were stabled and the steaks were sizzling.

'It's a good job you weren't lying about this place, like you were about the hills. If you had have been, you'd have been wearing my bike.'

'As if you could lift it in your state. I thought I'd lost you back there.'

'Yeah. There was a point when I was struggling with any slight incline, even speed bumps.'

'And flat bits.'

'Those too. Cheers, mate.'

'To the wind changing.' We clinked glasses. I didn't want to mention it, but if it was as strong the next day, we'd never make it to Huntingdon in time for our lift.

The steaks arrived, and another pint. And another. The pub dogs, Charlie and Nelson, circled our table for scraps. Another Charlie, a local non-league referee, arrived for last orders and launched into some tales of his time with the whistle. He regaled us with the time he had pinned Crawley boss Steve Evans, then manager of Stamford, to the wall by his throat for having called Charlie a cheat. This was a story everyone could relate to and delight in. I looked around the room to realise that nobody else was listening. Liz and Chris were closing down the bar. The dogs were curled up asleep in front of the fire. As was Will.

As we rolled slowly away the next day, weighed down by a Chris Special of a breakfast, we both broke out into huge grins. The wind had spun around 180 degrees to massage our backs instead of maul our faces. We whizzed through Stamford, by-passed Peterborough and flew down the old Great North Road alongside the A1 all the way to Huntingdon. We were supping pints in the Samuel Pepys before Sam had finished work.

Once the dash up and down the A1 for the Wimbledon match was out of the way, Will and I bade Sam farewell and carried on in the same vein. The following wind had rejuvenated Will to the extent that he made a lone breakaway in the Cambridgeshire countryside, the peloton only managing to catch up with him because he stopped for a cup of tea in Royston. It was warm as well as breezy, and my pale arms were beginning to burn. We stopped in a village to buy sun cream, realising after we'd splashed it all over us that what we'd bought was some kind of coconut tanning oil. We spent the rest of the day slowly cooking. And we stank like melted Bounty bars.

An extended, boozy lunch in a Hertfordshire pub gave us enough momentum to propel us right through Essex to the Thames. Feeling good, we decided to carry on into Kent before stopping for the night. We took the Dartford Crossing taxi, fortunately driven by a different guy this time. Once in Kent we began to flag. We had covered well over ninety miles and needed to find somewhere in the urban sprawl to camp.

A few miles further south, we wandered into the Castle Hotel in Eynsford and talked them into letting us pitch our tents in the beer garden. The pub was pretty full for karaoke night and we traipsed through the packed bar, feeling the locals' eyes burning into our lycra-clad backs. Pretty uncomfortable, but we could make it more so. *Just wait till the tents are up and we come back to sing for you.* The last time Will and I had sung karaoke together was fifteen years before, when we disgusted the locals in a rough Dundee pub with a heartfelt rendition of the Grease classic *Summer Nights*. I had been Sandy to Will's Danny, and we had been lucky to get away without being lynched.

We survived the night at the Castle and spent a fun half-hour in the morning roaming around the ruins of the Norman castle opposite the pub. We only had fifty miles to do before hitting the south coast. If all went to plan, we'd be in Eastbourne a day ahead of schedule. It was still a tough day, made even tougher by taking hilly backroads in a bid to stay off the A roads. I could already hear Will's inevitable cry of 'you've brought us to the highest place for miles around'.

He got the chance to trot it out a few times as we rolled on through pleasant hills dotted with oast houses, their white-tipped conical roofs pointing perkily into the sky like upturned Cornettos. Will saved the biggest moan of the day for Crowborough, where a sign at the top of the long main drag into town proclaimed it as the highest town in south-east England. We climbed that hill slowly enough to be able to eavesdrop on the conversations of the school kids walking alongside us. But at least we were now in Sussex, and a two-hour dash on the main roads brought us to the seaside. After a sweaty hug to mark the achievement, we flung the tents up in time for a romantic sunset stroll along the beach to the harbour where Will treated us to fish and chips. He had been a perfect gentleman for the entire trip, if you ignored the canvas-threatening farts he produced to punctuate my sleep.

We got to Eastbourne Borough's Priory Lane ground soon after they'd opened up. It's a neat little stadium with a low-slung clubhouse attached to one corner, giving it the feel of a village sports club. Which is pretty much what it is. Originally Langney FC, later Langney Sports, the club had been formed by a group of veterans unhappy that they had nowhere else to play. Their club had risen from parks football in the 1960s to one step away from the Football League. The previous season had been Borough's first at this level, and they had comfortably stayed up. This time round, they were suffering from the footballing equivalent of the difficult second album, and were fighting hard against relegation. The club's mere involvement in this league is incredible; it is traditionally thought of as the third-biggest club in the town, and neither Eastbourne United nor Eastbourne Town have ever competed this high up the pyramid.

The club officials knew we were coming and by what means, so they made sure everyone in the clubhouse looked after us. We were offered a continuous stream of pints, the first of which washed down our breakfast. By the time the rest of the City fans arrived, we were already very drunk. Fortunately, so were they. Quite a few of the southern contingent had piled off the train for a few pints in Brighton, and those who hadn't had clearly been drinking on the train.

There was an end-of-season, festival feel to the day. It had been designated a retro shirt match and many of the York supporters had squeezed themselves into long-forgotten jerseys in a variety of colours, accentuated by the bright sunshine. Clutching our pints under clear blue skies, chatting to friends old and new, the common bond of what had brought us all here really did shine through. Of course there are various factions amongst the support and not everyone sees eye-to-eye, but putting these petty grievances aside, us York City fans really are a magnificent lot.

At some point just before kick-off, Will put his arm round my shoulder and said, 'There's no way you're setting off tonight.'

'You mean there's no way we're setting off tonight?'

A huge grin of relief spread across his whiskery chops. 'You know what, mate? I think I might just take the train.'

'Fair enough. You'd only slow me down anyway.'

And it was fair enough. Will had planned to pedal back with me as far as London before going back to work, but I couldn't begrudge him an easy end to his holiday. With barely any preparation he had done phenomenally well, not only keeping pace with me most of the way, but forging ahead towards the end. Our drunken release at the end of the trip had left me in the exact situation the bending of the rules around the Wimbledon match was meant to avoid. By the time my hangover cleared in the morning, I would have two-and-a-half days to get back to York for the home match against Barrow. Without even trying, Will had succeeded in making the challenge even harder for me.

I usually have one or two pints before York matches – it helps to numb the pain – but I had never been this drunk at kick-off. I even tried to start my first chant since my teenage years. When Eastbourne's 'keeper Danny Knowles stooped down in front of us to retrieve the ball from against the hoardings, I was mildly surprised to hear myself roaring out:

'You're shit, and you're Knowles, you are!'

I roared alone. Not a soul joined in. Not even Will, who had been specifically primed to do so. There were one or two groans, a couple of appreciative nods from the front and a smile and a clap from Knowles himself. Well, I wouldn't be trying that again.

The York players started as if they had been in the bar with the fans. Two unmarked chances for Crabb and Atkin gave Borough a 2-0 lead after fifteen minutes. A third was ruled out for offside shortly afterwards. Little matter, as Atkin added it just after the half-hour. With our place in the play-offs assured, a certain amount of winding down had to be expected, but this was shambolic. The farce continued right up to just before half-time. Rankine was felled in the box for a soft penalty and refused to give the ball to Brodie. The strike partners got themselves into an unseemly scrap, tugging at the ball like baby girls fighting over a doll. Rankine won out and, fortunately for him, struck the ball firmly home for what was surely a consolation goal.

A big chunk of the York following didn't bother to come out for the second half, choosing instead to watch the Grand National in the bar. A wise decision, as the score remained 3-1 at the end. Will and Sando spent the entire second half sitting on the back step of the terrace, discussing Will's journey down and Sando's imminent trip.

As the York players were trooping past us to the coach afterwards, Martin Foyle came over to our group and apologised that we'd come all this way for such an abject performance. He even gave us a ball for a boozy kick-about. Once that petered out, Will and I put our tents up on the training pitch and weaved our way back to the harbour for food and more drink. Back at the club a couple of hours later, we were greeted like old friends. The home fans and officials were in great spirits after the win, which had significantly improved their chances of avoiding the drop. We became embroiled in another karaoke night, which turned into a lock-in.

I left Will at the station around midday and dribbled on for a measly forty-one miles until the strangely-named village of Plaxtol in Kent. A pint in the Papermakers Arms yielded the knowledge of the best place to put up my tent, in a park that ran down to the River Bourne. I woke at dawn on Monday with the awful realisation that, thanks to getting hammered in Eastbourne, I still had 250 miles to do by 7.45pm the following day. I'd given myself a three-day hangover.

I could do little else but get my head down. Raising it in the late afternoon, I was mildly pleased to find myself once again in Cambridgeshire. Whilst pondering a realistic target end-of-day target, I remembered that I knew a man with a caravan. Duncan had offered me a bed for the night in the unlikely event of me passing by again. He can't have been expecting me, but was as good as his word. The interior was much cleaner than the outside. It held a huge comfy bed and little else. It was perfect. I went to bed early and rose at 5am. Four hours later, I was in Sleaford, still ninety miles from York. My legs were in good shape and I was aided by a co-operative wind. I knocked the miles off with ease, getting to York well before kick-off. I wouldn't have subjected Will to the ordeal, but the fitness I'd gained over the season meant that cycling from the South Coast to North Yorkshire in two-and-a-half days had been surprisingly easy.

Two home games against Barrow and Grays were all that stood in the way of Sando getting back on a bike for the first time in a quarter of a century. Grays had already been relegated and Barrow were struggling to avoid joining them. Barrow's heavy-legged performance was testament to their continued involvement in the FA Trophy and the subsequent fixture congestion. A brace of Brodie headers and a well-taken goal from substitute Gash were the headlines in a routine 3-0 victory.

The day before the Grays match, news began to filter through that John Batchelor had died at the age of fifty-one from liver failure. His alcoholism had been quite well hidden, so it came as a shock to many. The unexpected news caused little sadness amongst York fans, and was even met with suspicion. Proof was required of the demise of a man whose every word had smacked of insincerity. I texted Will with the news. His immediate reply would have been echoed by York fans up and down the country: *How can you be sure?*

Perhaps understandably, the match against Grays was played in a strange atmosphere. Sporadic anti-Batchelor chants broke out throughout the match, some of them quite breathtaking in their rancour. There was a definite split in the Longhurst stand between those moved enough to sing songs revelling in a man's death, and those who thought this was a step too far, regardless of what he'd done to the club. I fell into the latter camp, but realised that my fine moral line had been drawn in shifting sands. Fifteen years ago, I would have probably been joining in with the chants of *this is what you get, when you fuck with us*. When Douglas Craig goes, the spiteful songs will be sung by many more people, and as hypocritical as this sounds, justifiably so.

Whether or not the terrace tumult transferred itself to the pitch is difficult to assess. It was certainly another curious, lethargic game between the two sides. Grays' cobbled-together team of kids and journeymen were playing for nothing but pride. York's final position was still to be determined: we would play either a fast-finishing Luton or an Oxford side reeling from the loss of the title to Stevenage.

Grays' plight worsened midway through the first half when goalkeeper Glyn Garner was sent off for hauling down Brodie, who missed the resultant penalty. He made amends at the start of the second half, firing past Garner's replacement Edwards from the edge of the area. Nothing else of note happened until Ingham punched an injury-time free-kick onto the boot of Reynolds, who blasted home an unlikely equaliser. Somewhere in rural France, my Dad tutted.

'Mum, this is...this is...' *Maybe I'll just have to say Sando.* I fished around for a name like a second-rate psychic. 'Ian?'

We'd known each other for more than a year, but I don't think I'd ever referred to Ian as anything other than Sando. In contrast, he's one of the few people who call me by my full first name. I savour the strangely formal tone.

We had met that morning at Bootham Crescent, and had already completed three or four gruelling miles to Bishopthorpe, where our feeding station was laden with bacon butties and cups of tea.

Suitably refreshed, we pushed on into Sando's first bike ride for twenty-five years. We crossed the River Ouse at Naburn and rolled along the now well-worn cycle track to Selby, where we holed up in a Sam Smith's pub.

'How are you holding up so far?'

'Really well. I'm enjoying this. I haven't felt this free in ages.'

A colleague had been causing him a few problems at work, and when we met at the Crescent he'd been in a distracted, slightly fractious mood. The glorious weather and sheer pleasure of cycling had helped him to cast off this mood off like a snake shedding its skin. Understandably nervous before the ride, within a few miles he had settled into a carefree rhythm. Somewhere north of Selby he had even changed his jeans for shorts.

'I'm glad you're enjoying it, I was worried you were going to resent the whole trip.'

He had been a bit jittery on the roads in town, so the bike track had been the perfect way to ease him into the trip.

'Don't get me wrong, I'm way out of my comfort zone here, but Lovejoy's helping.'

'Lovejoy?'

He patted the crossbar of his brand-new Specialized like a showjumper congratulating his horse after a clear round.

'I needed inspiration for what lies ahead. Lovejoy always pushed at the boundaries of cool and came out the other side a winner. It was meant to be.'

I had to admit a certain pang of jealousy. Neither the Ridgeback nor the Kona had acquired nicknames, and Sando had snaffled the best 1980s TV name. I could hardly start calling the Kona Bergerac or Morse. The-bike-with-no-name and I rolled along beside Lovejoy and Sando for another four hours before we decided to stop in Epworth to cap an easy forty-five mile day.

For the first time since I'd left Oxford eight months ago, I actually had some time to spare while on the road. We had a week to get to Stevenage, which meant we could ease Sando into the swing of it and do a bit of sight-seeing along the way. On a Lincolnshire B road we stumbled across the village of Stow and its Minster. The huge, imposing church completely dominates the village; it had served as the main church and administrative centre for this part of Lincolnshire until Lincoln Cathedral was built after the Norman invasion. After a pleasant half-hour poking about, we meandered off for the rest of the afternoon until we reached Leadenham, where we stopped for a pint in The Willoughby Arms to recover from the ride up the Ridgeway. When Sando came back from the bar with a second pint, it became clear that we would be stopping for the night as well. By this point of the season, I was skint and happy to camp everywhere, but Sando insisted on paying for the rooms and most of the meals. Adding in the cost of the bike, clothing and assorted paraphernalia, it had been a pretty expensive bet to lose.

Back at our table, Sando carried on a conversation with one of the regulars. Bob, a young local farmer, was telling us in his calm, matter-of-fact way, what we could see in the region.

'Well there's the Knight's Temple, up on the heath.'

'As in the Knights Templars?'

'Yep.'

'Fantastic. How do we get there?'

Bob explained with great patience the relatively straightforward route from pub to temple. Despite his detailed directions, within a few minutes of setting off in the morning we were hopelessly lost. The heath was treeless and almost featureless, apart from an occasional farm and a few disused WWII airfields – according to Bob, the bombers had returned safely to base by lining up their wing-tip with Leadenham church spire. We had no such navigator tricks up our sleeves, spending the morning trawling back and forth across rutted tracks dotted with pools and fallen trees, like a slowed-down version of the *Kick Start* opening credits. Scratching our heads down a narrowing farm track, we resorted to Sando's iPhone. After a bit of scrolling about, Temple Farm appeared on the map. We grinned at each other. He re-checked the screen and it was gone: were the Templars on to us?

About ready to give up the search, we pushed on until the dirt track met the tarmac. Amazingly, a little wooden sign at the side of the road pointed to Temple Farm. We pedalled through the yard, rounding a corner to be greeted by the sight of the magnificently restored thirteenth-century tower. Considering that the tower is almost completely intact, and one of the few tourist attractions for miles around, it is incredibly badly signposted. You get the feeling that the locals like it that way. Either that, or the shadowy, secretive Knights Templars prefer it not to be found.

As our eyes adjusted to finding what we'd spent all morning searching for, our ears were assaulted with a horrific keening, sobbing wail which seemed to be coming directly from the tower. It felt like we had cycled into an Umberto Eco novel, or one of the more sinister *Scooby Doo* episodes. I climbed the steep temple steps and pushed open the door with genuine trepidation.

The screams subsided as we entered the cool of the building. Inside, it was eerily quiet. Leaded windows cast a latticework light on the stone floor. A solitary chair had been placed in a corner, as if awaiting Van Gogh. A spiral staircase led upwards from the opposite corner. We climbed to the top, from where we could see out over the domain of the old church compound, of which only this tower remains. Where the church once stood was now a series of stables, one of which housed a noisy pack of black and tan foxhounds, wailing and screaming against their captivation.

The afternoon saw us easing our way through Lincolnshire's quiet, rolling hills until we stopped for the night at the Griffin. Shorter days in the saddle and a vast improvement in the weather meant that Sando avoided all of the problems that Will had encountered on our slog to Irnham. Putting our bags in our room, I noticed an odd sock lying on the bedside table. I must have left it there when Will and I had stayed; its partner was languishing alone in the bottom of my pannier, but thanks to Liz's thoughtfulness in washing and leaving it there, they could be reunited at last.

We had so much time on our hands that we completed a loop of Rutland Water the next day, ending up at Sando's friend Simon's house just north of Peterborough. Another stress-free day under Magritte skies brought us to Sam's in Huntingdon, where we stayed for the night before setting off for Stevenage. He had talked several of his colleagues and friends into riding with us, some of whom were actual proper cyclists. They coped well with our laughably slow pace and sportsman's breakfast of beer and sausage rolls.

Will had cycled from London that morning, and we got to Stevenage at roughly the same time. He had inadvertently treated himself to a selection of Hertfordshire's vantage points along the way, reluctantly conceding that keeping on the flat was trickier than it looked.

The bar at Broadhall Way was packed, as you would expect it to be before a match when the home side would be crowned as champions. A huge roar went up as Ledley King equalised for Spurs at Old Trafford on the big screens. When Stevenage was first designated a New Town, it became home to a huge influx of North Londoners; the wall of noise that greeted Spurs' short-lived parity was unsurpassed by any cheers for Stevenage's winning goal or coronation.

A 1-0 victory for the home side was to be expected. David Bridges' first-half strike was enough to beat a York side who, like most of their supporters, were already concentrating on the two-legged play-off against Luton. After the final whistle, and Stevenage's strangely muted celebrations, we took celebratory photos over a couple of pints in the least-bad pub we could find, then made our way to the station. Sando would return to work with a seemingly sincere promise to commute on Lovejoy from time to time. I would go back to Will's for a couple of days' rest before making my way back to York for the last time. As we stashed our bikes on the train, I was struck by an idle realisation: I had achieved what I'd set out to do.

The journey from Stevenage to York would be my last unaccompanied ride of the whole adventure. Another southern City exile, Dave, had finally come good on his season-long promise to ride a leg with me, committing to ride from York to Luton for the second leg of the play-offs. If by some miracle we got through to the final, I was sure to have company on the short hop from Luton to Wembley.

I spent a bit longer than expected in London, so had to complete my last solo mission in style. A short ride and overnight stop in Huntingdon served as an appetiser for the main course: I had decided to attempt the longest trek of the entire trip, from Huntingdon to York in a day.

Sam acted as a fantastic lead-out man, setting a metronomic pace. Fourteen miles after one hour, twenty-eight after two. He turned for home near Peterborough with a broad smile on his face. There would be no Walwyn sightings today. Left to my own devices, my pace dipped a little, but I kept up a decent rhythm. Forty-one miles after three hours, fifty-four after four, sixty-seven after five. I was just south of Lincoln by 2pm, less than half-way home.

I had a radio interview at 3pm, so decided to get myself comfy in a beer garden which turned out to be a wise decision. I've no idea how, but in getting off the bike I gashed my shin to the bone on the serrated edge of the pedal. The landlady kindly gave me a huge bag of ice to press against the wound. A kindness I repaid by trailing blood through her pristine bar. I had been extremely fortunate to get this far without being stopped by injury or illness. I thought of Ian from the Banbury campsite, his knee ruptured a mere week into his trip, and raised my second pint to him.

Numbed by ice and cider, I got gingerly back on and set my sights on York for the last time. I savoured every pedal-turn of the journey, revelled in the solitude, marvelled at the sheer perfection of the bicycle. I took the map out of the handlebar bag and stuck it in one of the panniers. I was going to cycle the eighty-odd miles home by memory, as if returning from a trip to the shops.

The road out of Lincoln took me through Saxilby, where Will and I had stopped for lunch on the way to Eastbourne, posing with a pub regular's garden gnome that was painted in Lincoln City colours. On past Stow, where Sando and I had explored the Minster; alongside Sturgate airfield, where Will and I had once sought shelter from the remorseless wind; over the River Trent at Gunness where a precise pigeon had spattered Will's shoulder; along the most perfect little road that shadows the A18; through Thorne and Selby to a midnight bath and bed. A 150-mile day undertaken with relative ease, a distance I wouldn't have even contemplated at the start of the season. You know when people do something strenuous and then say they are ready to go again? Well, I could barely walk, let alone carry on. But I'd done it once, and that was enough.

The Jorvik Reds are a group of late-teenage to early-twenties York supporters almost entirely responsible for creating any kind of atmosphere at home games. Congregating in the middle of the Longhurst, their chants are often met with apathy from surrounding fans but they carry on regardless. I'm one of the guilty mumblers – oh, I used to sing, but, you know...

The JRs excelled themselves for the first leg of the play-offs. Correctly assessing that the players would need all the help they could get against an arguably stronger Luton side, they placed red and blue cards on each seat, armed themselves with an Andrex lorry-load of toilet roll and sang their bloody hearts out. Prior to kick-off, I had been rattling buckets outside the turnstiles for the Alzheimer's Society (when I asked for permission at the start of the season the charity slots had all been snapped up, so I optimistically bagged a home play-off match). I squeezed into a packed Longhurst Stand just in time to see the players come out to a wall of sound, a sea of red and blue in the stands and a bog roll ticker-tape reception. You could see them grow taller as they strode out to the centre circle.

Almost from the first whistle, Luton took control of the match. Heslop and Keane dominated the midfield, piercing York's defence with a series of through-balls. Ingham was called into action time and time again to pull off a series of smart saves from Gallen, Gnakpa, Craddock and Howells. At the other end, Tyler was not tested at all until after half-time. Even then, he had a simple save to make from Graham's header. Sensing a priceless away win, the 1,200 who had made the trip up from Bedfordshire started to make themselves heard.

Luton pressed and bullied, trying to turn their obvious supremacy into goals. At the back, Graham and McGurk swayed, but did not buckle. With only a few minutes left, disaster struck. Craddock dropped the ball onto Gnakpa's laces, six yards out. McGurk and Graham were nowhere. Ingham was nowhere. Gnakpa lashed a venomous volley. Straight over the bar. Right out of the ground.

As the game wound down, defiant cries of 'We. Are. York.' rang out from all sides of the ground. The JRs display and sustained singing had even roused the Main Stand regulars from their customary slumber. We had taken a battering here, and a 0-0 draw was a decent result. A slender something to work on at Kenilworth Road. As the ref prepared to blow his whistle, Rankine headed an innocuous flick-on in the general direction of the goal. Shane Blackett seemed to slip, and headed the ball up in the air instead of back to his 'keeper. Brodie, who had been marked out of the game by Blackett all night, nipped in behind him to toe-poke a half-volley from the edge of the area. The ball flew just inside Tyler's left-hand post, coming to rest on a bed of unfurled toilet rolls in the back of the net.

Delirium.

MAY

Over the course of the previous nine months I had stayed overnight in many spur of the moment locations. The latest and last of these stays would be in the beer garden of the Rose & Crown in Tilton, Leicestershire. Dave and I flung up our tents and made our way inside for sustenance. It had to be the last impromptu night of shelter, as the following day we would aim for Luton and stay with a mate of Dave's in Harpenden, also Dave. It would either be the last day's cycling, or the penultimate. The season and the trip would either end in ignominy in Bedfordshire, or in a tilt at glory at Wembley.

Dave and Sando have been close friends since childhood, and maintain a healthy rivalry still visible at Monday night football in Brixton. Sando had clearly won this round of battles. His trip had been a carefree jaunt under sunny skies, with no particular place to go. Dave and I had some serious miles to cover in blustery drizzle, and I kept taking us to places with names like Tilton-on-the-Hill. Coming at the end of a tough day, it was a drag of a climb up to the Rose and Crown. As a boy, Sir David Attenborough used to pedal these very lanes to uncover the local fossils and ammonites, but this was of scant interest to Dave. He simply wanted to crest the hill alive, not inspect its innards.

We had set off that morning from Worksop, where we had spent an eye-opening Friday night wandering round town in slack-jawed wonder at the slack-jawed wonders. It had been a sobering evening spent watching crowds of blank-eyed zombies shuffle from pub to grim pub. We were starving, but couldn't find an open restaurant in a town of 40,000 souls. A promising-looking Mexican joint had recently closed down; an Indian was closed due to staff illness; the pubs had stopped serving food: there was nowhere to eat other than kebab shops and chippies. The air hang heavy with a stench of badly-cooked meat and a real sense of menace. If nothing else, it was good preparation for Kenilworth Road.

The day's ride from Worksop to Tilton had been a tough one, and was followed by another. We spoke little as we battled with wave after wave of strength-sapping hills, gritting our teeth up the finest inclines Leicestershire, Northamptonshire and Bedfordshire had to offer. We struggled over the last one into Luton just as it got dark, crawling wearily through darkening streets to take a desultory snap in front of the gates at Kenilworth Road. Without knowing if it would be the last ride and last game, I felt nothing but ambivalence.

It was the eve of the match, and we could pedal no further. Dave's mate "Also Dave" had been drinking so couldn't give us a lift. All London-bound trains were suspended. The replacement coaches' holds were not big enough to accommodate two bikes. We somehow crammed them into the back of a cab and folded ourselves in beside them. If this were to be the end of the trip, it was a fittingly farcical one.

Having already visited the ground, we had no cycling to do on the day of the match, so had a couple of pre-match pints in Harpenden to calm the nerves. An equally twitchy Luton fan paced up and down outside, cigarette and pint in one hand, straw boater in the other.

We joined Sando, Will, Sam and the rest at Kenilworth Road and funnelled in through the quirky terrace house turnstile. The place was packed with 10,000 noisy fans, most of them sporting Luton's white and orange. Haydn was in there somewhere. His men set the pace early on, with McGurk and Ingham forced into sharp action to repel decent chances for Tom Craddock. The same man pulled another good chance wide shortly afterwards. As expected, we were under the cosh. Luton had to score just to restore parity in the tie, which meant they had to force the pace. Ingham and his resolute defence held firm throughout the first half. It had been a horribly tight forty-five minutes, as much fun to watch as the previous day's hills had been to climb. We had more of this to come in the second half – Foyle's men were used to holding out for a 1-0 win over ninety minutes; it looked like he had set them up to try the same over 180.

This notion was disproved two minutes after the restart. Carruthers was tripped right on the edge of the Luton box. Rankine struck a low, fizzing free-kick that Tyler could only push back out to Carruthers himself, who bundled it over the line. Silence from three sides of the ground, unbridled joy in the end that mattered.

Luton now had to score two more goals in one half of football than they'd managed in the previous three. Accustomed as we are to York messing things up from almost any conceivable position, a mood of cautious optimism prevailed. Nascent 'Wemb-er-ley' chants were quickly shushed down. This was a lead too precious to jinx.

Foyle withdrew his troops even deeper, in anticipation of Luton's renewed attacks. The home side had no option other than to fling everything they had at us, but our defence simply looked increasingly solid, and their attacks increasingly desperate. Proof that we would not lose came with fifteen minutes to go. Craddock broke free of the York defence for a clear run on goal. As he prepared to fire past Ingham for the equaliser, McGurk appeared from nowhere to slide in and execute a tackle as elegant as Bobby Moore's on Pelé at the 1970 World Cup. Seemingly outpaced, McGurk had made up a couple of yards on Craddock to make a lunge which, had its timing been even slightly out, would have meant a sure-fire penalty and red card. With impeccable timing, he hooked his leg round Craddock's to force the ball out of play. This time, the 'Wemb-er-ley' chants were allowed to gather volume.

In the dying seconds, Luton's full-back Adam Newton allowed his frustration to get the better of him, getting sent off with a neat little kick-the-ball-away/foul-mouth-tirade one-two. As the final whistle confirmed our 1-0 victory, some of the Luton fans followed his lead, spilling on to the pitch and advancing on the celebrating York players, who took cover from a shower of coins and other debris in the stand with their fans. For a split-second, it seemed as if the Luton fans would wade in after them, but their advance was quickly closed down by a line of stewards as effective as McGurk's wonder tackle.

Once the cordon was in place, a couple of hundred more of Luton's less brave wannabe-thugs lined up behind it to throw coins and insults from a safe distance. Ugly scenes for sure, but hardly the rebirth of hooliganism a titillation-starved media subsequently portrayed it as.

A week later, I had one of those moments on the trip where I wondered what the hell I was playing at. I was waiting at St Albans train station for a forumer named spasy paddy (another lower-case fan) to arrive to ride the last leg to Wembley with me. When he arrived, it quickly became apparent that we'd both made a huge mistake. He turned up on a carbon road bike, dressed in full Sky team kit, and proceeded to take the piss out of my bike, my kit, my bags, my hair, my team and my face. All fair targets of course, but you need to be a very accurate shot when you're a Barnet-supporting midget David Baddiel lookalike. spasy is a proper club cyclist, used to eating up the miles as quickly as possible. He made no concession for the extra gear I was carrying or the slightly sentimental nature of this particular leg of the trip. He just flounced off in a combative huff, dropping back every few miles to list my inadequacies.

I had spent the week leading up to the play-off final at Jola's, deep in enemy territory. In the other semi-final, Oxford had comfortably beaten Rushden & Diamonds 3-1 on aggregate to lend the season a pleasingly-symmetrical feel. After that opening-day defeat at the Kassam Stadium, few would have predicted York to make it this far. Oxford would go into the final as slight favourites, having been the better side over the course of the season, and having finished as strongly as we had. When the week off drew to a close, I went back to London to collect my bike and take the train to Luton to pick up the trail for the last time.

The trains all stopped at St Albans, which gave spasy and me an extra twenty-two miles in each other's company. We did an about-turn at Kenilworth Road and got into a more companionable rhythm as we rolled on towards London. It became apparent that he wasn't a bad bloke at all, just needlessly competitive. In truth, I should have pedalled these last few miles either alone or with close friends. With the end of the adventure nigh, I was in a weird mood, which was hardly spasy's fault. We sped along, quickly finding ourselves engulfed by North London's outer reaches. We pedalled down Wembley Way together a few times for Yorkshire TV cameras, took a photo and shook hands goodbye.

I took my chances by locking the Kona to the bike racks. At almost all the other matches I'd been to, a shed or an office or a corner of the ground had been found for the bike. At Altrincham I lashed it to a terrace barrier, at Barrow and Salisbury it went in the club gym, at York it was always stored in the shop's stockroom. Only at Mansfield had I failed to find a spot to stash it, but in fairness, iron horse sightings still tend to overawe folk round there. But there was nowhere in Wembley's vast acreage of tunnels, cellars and conference rooms for me to leave it. Why? *'Health and safety, mate.'*

Spurred on by the rare opportunity to see their heroes run out at a four-sided stadium, the Oxford fans had snapped up 35,000 tickets. As we took our place amongst the less showy 10,000 York fans, it was impossible not to be impressed by the yellow and blue hordes that had turned the opposite end into a raucous Con-Lib coalition party. At several points throughout the match they filled the whole stadium with an impressive and hostile noise.

Their team was quicker into tackles and quicker out of the blocks. The York players were stunned by the opening onslaught, and by the time they had woken up and realised what was happening, it was almost too late.

A defence which had performed superbly all season chose the biggest possible stage on which to succumb to nerves. Perhaps spooked by the dithering in front of him, Ingham took it upon himself to rush off his line three times in the opening half-hour. On fifteen minutes, he dashed to the edge of his area but Constable beat him to the ball and hooked it on to Green who smashed an unstoppable shot into the vacant net. The second time, Ingham had been left exposed and had little choice but to leave his line. Constable beat him with ease.

Numbed disbelief was written across the faces of City fans all around. We were 2-0 down with barely twenty minutes played. I thought of Rupert celebrating in the other end and took a petulant left-foot swing at my pannier, connecting with the same part of my foot that had crashed into a Kassam seat on the opening day. Well, I hardly needed it for cycling any more.

Midson should have added a third shortly afterwards, when Ingham flapped at a corner to present him with a free header, which he smacked against the post. We hadn't taken a battering like this all season. Ingham was prone to the occasional rush of blood, and they had seemed to be more frequent this season, but it had been an incongruously shaky campaign for him. A year before, his saves had practically kept us in this league, and in most matches he had made one or two goal-sparing saves. He wasn't solely to blame anyway. It seemed particularly cruel for the defence to be having a collective off-day when it mattered most.

Could Foyle inspire his men to turn this round? They had to get through to half-time first. Just before the break, we scored. Purkiss' hopeful centre was fumbled by Oxford 'keeper Clarke, who somehow managed to propel the ball over his own line with his hands and face. Maybe it was an act of goalkeeping solidarity. Whatever it was, it was 2-1 at half-time. Hope coursed anew through York fans and players alike.

York attacked towards their own supporters with intent from the start of the second half, driven on by the probing Lawless. Ten minutes after the restart, the big moment arrived. A friendly ricochet deposited the ball at Rankine's feet ten yards out. Here came the equaliser. Rankine placed it firmly, calmly, wide of Clarke in the Oxford net. And quite a bit wide of the goal. The collective groaning and holding of heads underlined how good a chance it had been.

Undeterred, we pressed on in search of an equaliser. Lawless hit a hopeful twenty-five-yarder just over, Barrett dragged a shot wide, Brodie shot tamely at Clarke. Courtney Pitt, on as a substitute, blasted another header at Clarke, who made a smart save. The volume in the York end was rising, the pressure mounting on the Oxford players. Their fans were even occasionally outsung. The clock ticked down, and still we pressed. With a couple of minutes left, we forced a precious corner, packing everyone into the box bar Ingham. Pitt struck the ball confidently, firmly, behind every single York player and straight into the path of an Oxford midfielder who immediately counter-attacked. It was one of the most despicably poor dead-ball strikes I had ever seen. Oxford broke with alacrity, with only Lawless in a position to get back to help Ingham. The attack was as ruthless as it was swift, and left Alfie Potter with as much time as he liked to pick his spot to make it 3-1.

Well, that was that.

Oxford had deserved to be promoted, both on the day and over the course of the season. A sizeable portion of the York contingent stayed behind to acknowledge this fact by clapping the Oxford team off the pitch as well as their own. But the applause rang hollow. We had been nearly good enough to clamber out of a poor league. The bar had been set quite low, but we had still managed to knock it off with a trailing leg. Failure is easy to deal with; it's the fleeting sniff of success that kills you. I'd rather we had finished seventeenth.

York fans have disappointment hard-wired into their DNA. We are supporters of a very occasionally mildly successful lower-league team. We're used to drudgery, disaster and defeat: an unholy trinity that suits us and sometimes hurts us, like a snazzy pair of shoes half a size too small.

So why let us get so close? Why raise our hopes like this only to dash them? Why bring us to the national stadium to humiliate us on national TV? Why, when all hope is just about extinguished, resurrect those fragile hopes by tossing us an unlikely lifeline which we would inevitably fail to grasp?

Just let us finish seventeenth; it's so much less painful that way.

As things begin to unravel for John Cleese's character Brian Stimpson in *Clockwise*, he sits down in the middle of a country lane, wailing '*It's not the despair, I can take the despair. It's the hope I can't stand*'. At least he was out in the open fields with only one of his students for company. I felt exactly the same, but had to plot an escape through the yellow-thronged streets surrounding Wembley and cycle to Ealing to meet the gang.

Back at Will's flat, we picked over the defeat. Raw sadness in time gave way to acceptance, which was shouldered out of the way by defiance. We would come back stronger next year. Wouldn't we?

Much later that evening, I pedalled the Kona from Ealing to Paddington where I met Jola. A fair few yellow-shirted revellers were still milling joyously around the station. We joined some of them on the platform and boarded a train to the city where we would write the next chapter of our lives.

Oxford.

One of the central characters in Georges Perec's *Life: A User's Manual*, a wealthy eccentric named Bartlebooth, chooses to commit fifty years of his life to an artistic project. Bartlebooth spends ten years learning to paint, then twenty years sailing round the world with his valet Smautf, stopping in a different port every fortnight to capture it in watercolour.

He sends each painting back to Winckler, a craftsman tasked with mounting each canvas on board and cutting it into an elaborate jigsaw. Bartlebooth eventually returns home to re-assemble the puzzles in the order he painted them, taking two weeks over each one. Once completed, they are treated with a chemical to rebind the canvas and removed from their backing. Bartlebooth sends the pictures back to the ports in which he had painted them, where the canvases are dipped in another solution to dissolve the paint, and destroyed. Bartlebooth falls behind schedule, goes blind and dies with an unfittable jigsaw piece in his hand.

His project is almost always interpreted as a flawed, futile one doomed to failure, which it turns out to be. But what should also be considered is that he dreamt up and tried to carry out something unique, he assembled a band of accomplices to help him live out his long-held dream and he experienced and recorded much of what the world has to offer.

Oxford had been my blank canvas, and would be so again.

What had I achieved over the course of the season? Something. Nothing much. We were still in the same god-awful league. But I had poked about in beautiful corners of this wonderful country that I otherwise may not have seen. I had been part of crowds that had exploded in rage and in joy. I had ridden solo and in company old and new: for Winckler and Smautf read Will and Sam, and many other companions; the finest one could wish for.

Across a lifetime, we all have hundreds of these blank canvases at our disposal, ready to be daubed in any way we see fit. And if you see fit to undertake an essentially futile, whimsical adventure such as painting and destroying canvases, or pedalling 10,000 miles according to the vagaries of a fixture list, then more power to your elbow. And you will meet beauty and heartache and glory along the way. And when it's over, you might find that what may have once seemed pointless whimsy has left traces on your canvas that are impossible to dissolve.

Go on, get out there, do something! Just make sure you follow a better team.

EPILOGUE

It's fair to say that it's taken a while to get this book to publication. Since Oxford's win at Wembley two-and-a-bit years ago, much has changed.

Sam and Will got married. Not to each other, to actual real-life women.

Lovejoy now lives in Sando's hallway and gets a daily pat on the saddle, if not a daily outing.

WBA Matt is still playing the ukulele, and still thinking about a similar bike trip following the Baggies.

Andy Ward finished his book on football and sociology, and called it *Football Nation*.

Rhinestone is back from his round-the-world trip, four years older and wiser. This April, I rode with many others on his last leg from Reading to Banbury. His book will probably be out before mine. spasy paddy rode with us that day, showing his true colours by doubling back to help me up a series of hills when I was plainly struggling. He performed this deed with exceptional good grace and without resorting to snarky comments, which this time would have been justified. He remains prone to an occasional flounce.

Jola and I had a daughter, which partly explains why it took me so long to complete the book.

Sometime last year, Mum sent me a cutting she had found when she was sorting through Gran's papers. It was an article from a 2005 copy of *The Evening Press*, looking back at sixty-odd years at Bootham Crescent. The top half of one page was taken up by a photo of the massed ranks in the Shipton Street end, part of the 28,000 crowd gathered to watch the 1938 FA Cup quarter-final against Huddersfield. In amongst the vast bank of mostly flat-capped supporters, a bare-headed man is picked out with a blue biro asterisk. My Grandad. It is definitely him, and it both warms and breaks my heart to think of my Gran sitting in her armchair, working along the tightly-packed rows of black and white faces until she found him, sixty-seven years after the match and twelve years after his death.

AFC Wimbledon beat Luton in the 2011 play-off final to complete their return to League football, one rung below Franchise FC. A few divisions below, Chester's phoenix club is rising through the leagues.

Rushden & Diamonds no longer exist. Near-neighbours Kettering took over their Nene Park home, leaving Rockingham Road to the developers. Huge cash injections have helped Crawley Town and Fleetwood Town, also-rans and never-beens, climb out of the Conference and into the Football League. Richard Brodie played a part in both promotions, having moved from York to Crawley, who then loaned him out to Fleetwood.

Martin Foyle was sacked part-way through the 2010-2011 season after a string of poor results culminated in a 5-0 thrashing at Mansfield. Gary Mills took over, steering his inherited squad to a place just outside the play-offs, despite their poor start to the campaign.

In his first full season in charge, he assembled a talented squad full of attacking intent who swashbuckled rather than bored their way to the play-offs, where they squeezed Mansfield out over two legs. They finished the season with two consecutive matches at Wembley, beating Newport County 2-0 in the first, the FA Trophy final.

In the play-off final a week later, Luton Town once more stood in the way. Luton took a first-minute lead. We wobbled, then simply outplayed them, scoring a blistering equaliser and a hugely offside winner. Tears that had been pent up over eight long years flowed all round at the final whistle. Tears of relief and redemption.

You tried to kill our club, Douglas Craig.

You failed.

Oh, Sal: remember when I stayed at yours on the way back from Poland? And I pedalled to the station to get a train to Stoke so I could pick up the trail again?
I just got on a train to York. I wasn't tired or injured or up against time or anything.
You wouldn't credit it, would you?

ACKNOWLEDGEMENTS

So many kind people helped me over the course of the ten months and beyond that my sieve-like mind is bound to have forgotten to thank some of them here. For that I can only apologise, and thank you all once again.

Thanks to Mum, Dad, Sal and Paul and their families.

To Andy Ward, without whose/who's/whom's help I would never have emerged blinking into the light.

To Garry Vaux, for taking this project on.

To Lee-Ann Donaldson, for her wonderful artwork.

To Michael Elgie, for his fantastic logo.

To Richard Herring, for reminding us all why York City are Magic.

To Paul Mulderrig, John at Cyclescene, Matthew Jones, Sam Smith, Will Martel, Ian Sanderson, John Douglas, Nick Bassett, Sophie Hicks, The Blake-Rhinestones, Ridgeback Arthur, Cycle Heaven Andy, Paul Elliot, Graham Bradbury, Frank Ormston, Josh Easby, Graham Titchener, Matt Sproston, Stuart Martel, Dave Flett, Gill Myers, Lisa McNaughton, Ian Tyssen, Helen Cooney, Molly Loyd, Adam Bilton, Gemma Colley, Dave McGrain, Antic Hay & The Master, Matilda Smith, Judith Hughes, Gavin Spowage, Graham and Jackie, Daniel Edwards, Jo Crabtree, Charlotte Johnson, James Grieve, Jo Curran, Paul Webb, Mike Bridge, Dave Hattee, Marcus Cerny, Dave Ward, Conrad Keating, Dot and Ray, Jim Waterson, Max Benson, Pete Brandon, Chris & Liz at the Griffin, Courtney & Tom, Pete Gill, Ian Stevens, Ian Hey, Johnny Burrell, Scott Blease, Matt Carroll, Malcolm et al at the School Boy in Norton, Kev at the Boot & Shoe in Ellerton, Russell Smith, Tony Farrelly, Sue & Keith at the Swallow's Nest, Adam & Gavin Rennison, Jack Hamblin, Sir Tom Finney, Steve Raw, Reverend Bunday, Joe O'Connor, Haydn Hamm, Helen & Gary, Chris Williams, Graham Lawton, Oliver Smith, Bob Davis, the owners of the Belmont Guest House in Tamworth, Duncan at the Globe, David Casey, Clive Brookes, Alex Edwards, Phil Richardson, Andrea Meneghelli, David Chadwick at Carradice, Andy James at Michelin, John Cookson at Exposure, Nikki Skinner at Rab, Steven Halsall, Rick Lovering, Chris Bradley, David Jack at Moore Large, Sharon Shortle, Archbishop John Sentamu, Andrew Barringer, Colin Burgess, Mark Hopkin, Andy Sallnow, Tim Fuell, Nick Holmes and Tony the welder, without whom the trip might have ended before it had really begun.

To forumers OldManKensey, Grifter, FurQ, moist, spasy paddy, Rhinestone, BifferSpice, Jigsaw, Myfanwy, Drdee, Adso of Melk and Shiva.

I Jola, oczywiście.